above
the
clouds

Mike
Moeller

Above the Clouds Ministries
Knoxville, TN

*To Cathy, my wife, who through our darkest days stood firm and
was the rock for our family. To Morgan, you are so strong and brave.
I love you, I am so proud of you, and we will be buddies forever.
To Casey, Kendall, and Luke, of whom I am so proud and who
made us laugh on our hardest days. I love you all so much.*

*To the Lord Jesus Christ, my Savior and my King.
I do not want to go through this again, but I thank you for refining me
through the fire and showing me what is truly important.
Thank you for rescuing my heart.*

Above the Clouds
The Miraculous Healing of a Little Girl
by Mike Moeller

Above the Clouds Ministries
P.O. Box 22715
Knoxville, TN 37933
www.abovethecloudsministries.net

Copyright © 2004
Cover and interior design © TLC Graphics, www.TLCGraphics.com

ISBN: 0-9758961-0-5
Printed in the United States of America

ACKNOWLEDGEMENTS

There are so many people to thank that we could not cover them all. To those not specifically mentioned: Thank you for your prayers, food, love, and support.

Julia Dalton (Cathy's mother), for moving in and taking care of the kids when we were not able. You were and are always there for us. We love you so much.

Betty Moeller (my mother). You have cried so much with us through it all. I now understand just a little how you felt when you lost Susan.

Gene "The Colonel" Moeller (my dad). You have left us to be with Jesus. But I want you to know how much I miss you. Thank you for being there for me. I can't wait to see you again.

Diane Conner (my sister). You were my hero in ICU. I love you!

Angela and Chris Dodd (Cathy's sister and brother-in-law). Angela, thank you for the runs each night and bringing laughter back into our home. Chris, you showed your love for us by coming to Knoxville to help out before you were part of the family.

Mike Dalton (Cathy's brother), for driving to the hospital just to sit with me one night.

The Bransons (Scott, Jill, Jonathan, Joshua, Jeremiah), our best friends. Thank you for your shoulders to cry on.

The Shofners (Mike, Janette, Tucker, Micalea, and soon to be Reef, Bay, and Natalia). You were always there for us. Thank you for taking care of Luke and Kendall in our darkest days.

Jeannie Hunter, for introducing us to the Holy Spirit and leading our Home Church. We love you so much!

Bill and Lisa Speigel and little Billy. We love you, and we hope and pray for the day little Billy is healed. You are such wonderful parents.

Anthony and Monica Scaff and Charlie. You have shown me many things. Thank you for sneaking Reese's Peanut Butter Cups to Morgan.

Kristin and Quinlan Lacy. We continue to pray for healing for Quinlan. We love you both.

West Town Christian Church, our family. You all have watched with us as God has healed Morgan. I will never forget your tears and applause as Morgan walked down the aisle.

George Clark and Ron Bull. Thank you for helping me face the toughest times and for trying to answer my toughest questions.

The Coverts (Craig, Rhonda, Janelle, Chad and Krista). Craig, thank you for just showing up one night for a walk, and Rhonda, for being our expert on diabetes. Janelle, you have no idea what you mean to our family.

Jared Ross. You are like my younger brother I never had. Thanks for hanging out with my dad in the consultation room.

Patty Chen, for just being there, for taking care of Luke, and for being willing to do anything for us.

Libby Gaylor, for caring for Morgan overnight and giving us some full nights of sleep.

Dr. Rick Glover (Morgan's pediatrician), for being there every day with us.

The Staff of East Tennessee Children's Hospital: Dr. Childs and staff and the many incredible nurses – Jackie, Bill, Gail.

Head nurse Karen Herbstritt, for the persistent daily feedings and the unique hair washings over the trash can. Thank you for helping us laugh.

Dr. Nichols and staff. Thank you Cathy VanOstrand for your energy and passion for a cure for this disease.

East Tennessee's Children's Rehab Center (Children's Corner): Lori, Jan, Karen, Jeanine, Robyn, Stacy, Katie, Gini, Julie, Helen, Susie, Ty, Kim and the rest of the staff. Thank you for your encouragement, support, and love for Morgan.

US LEC family: Gina, Chuck, Mark, Matthew, Heath, Rick, Hunter, Keith, and Jonathan. Thank you for crying with me when work didn't matter.

Love 89 radio station. Your daily Morgan update and the thousands upon thousands of prayers from your listeners. Jason McKay, we miss seeing you.

The Baileys: Mike, Kim, and McKenzie. Thank you for the steaks and for recommending Morgan for Dream Connection. McKenzie, you were Morgan's best friend through the good times and the bad.

Dream Connection, for making her dream come true – her second dream that is.

And to: Jesus Christ, the Great Physician!

And special thanks and gratitude to those who helped make this book a reality:

Jeff Williamson, who first read my notes and encouraged me to write the book. You helped me see that I could do this and stuck with me to the end. Thank you!

TLC Graphics, Tami and Erin, you both have done a fantastic job. From the cover to the inside, you made it fun and easy. God bless you!

And, finally, to Dick Christianson, my editor. I know that God made our paths cross. I wanted a man filled with the Spirit and who loves God to edit my book. You are such a man. I will never be able to thank you enough.

TABLE OF CONTENTS

INTRODUCTION

For the past couple years people have asked, "When are you going to write a book about Morgan?" I've decided it's time.

No, God has decided it's time.

I'm apprehensive about writing this book, not because the story of our daughter Morgan's miraculous healing (the therapists called her "Miracle Morgan") isn't worth telling, but because I want to make sure that the glory is all God's. I want to write the book for the right reasons – to tell Morgan's story, of course. But more important, I want to write the book to reveal how God has transformed our lives forever through the healing of our daughter.

Morgan's story is incredible. It's the kind of story you read and say, "Wow!" We certainly never expected anything like this to happen to us. But it did. It happened to the Moellers.

What's even more amazing, though, is how God has used Morgan to touch so many other people. Scott Branson, a close friend, said this: "Ministers and missionaries spend their entire life working for the Lord to change the lives of others. Yet here's a little girl who hasn't spoken a word and is changing people's hearts. Isn't God a mystery?"

Scott is so right.

Perhaps a visual image will help you better understand how God has changed lives through Morgan. Imagine that a meteorite crashes into a remote area of the Mojave Desert. It comes smashing to earth with little or no warning, wreaking havoc at the site of impact. But the result of the impact is also felt for miles in every direction as the ground shakes, buckles, and vibrates.

Morgan's illness was a lot like that. It came on without warning, devastated her physically and emotionally, and violently shook the lives of all those in her immediate family as well as those who only heard about her terrible trials. But even more than the illness, God's miraculous healing has shaken all of us. It has spiritually transformed and changed forever the lives of those closest to Morgan as well as the lives of others who have heard the story. In fact, as you read about God's miracle in Morgan's life and the life of her family, I believe you will feel the "ripple effect" as well. That's my prayer.

Since I had no thoughts of writing a book as all of this was unfolding, I didn't keep notes. Nevertheless, I know that God has revealed to me what to write. In addition to the narrative of events, God has had me record the "truths" He revealed to us along the way – truths that have strengthened my faith as well as truths that are leading us to have "life more abundantly." I pray that those truths will be revealed to you and that they will change your life forever as you read the story of "Miracle Morgan."

chapter one

CRUISIN' *with* *the* MOELLERS: FOR NOW

O ur doctor led us into one of the new private rooms to tell us about Morgan's condition. She had significant brain damage, and the damage to her brain stem was severe on the left side. I began crying out: "How could this have happened? Just a couple days ago she was running around playing, and now she has brain damage? This is my daughter! This is my little Morgan!"

I was overwhelmed and I dropped to my knees, put my head on Cathy's lap, and cried. Cathy was crying too, but she kept saying, "God has a plan. God has a plan." Cathy truly felt everything was going to work out. I wasn't so sure. For me, this was the worst day of my life. I begged and pleaded, "God take this burden from me."

To understand how God eventually used Morgan's illness to transform our family, you need to understand what our life was like before the onset of her illness in October of 2001. Put simply, the Moeller family was on cruise control. We were living the American dream. We had it all. I had a great job with a new start-up company in telecommunications. Cathy also had her dream job; she was a stay-at-home mom taking care of the kids (and working much harder than me).

The kids were in school and doing great. We went to church every Sunday. Cathy taught the Sunday-morning high school class, and I taught the middle school class. We were very happy and content. Life was really good.

But there was something inside me that knew this perfect lifestyle wouldn't last. Something was about to change. What I didn't know was that the change I was sensing would transform us forever.

Cathy had grown up in a Christian home with a younger sister and an older brother. She was a model daughter – beautiful, smart, and athletic to boot. Her parents loved each other very much. I still remember walking in on Ed and Julia as they were kissing in their kitchen. I was embarrassed, but I told myself then that I wanted to be part of this loving family.

Cathy asked the Lord to come into her life when she was only 8 years old. She had always known about Jesus, but this was when she committed publicly to being a follower of Christ. Cathy is almost four years younger than me (she reminds me of this often) and went to Farragut High School in Knoxville, Tennessee.

I was the youngest of three children and the only boy in the Moeller family. We were a career military family and moved around a lot. Dad, "the Colonel," as people knew him, was often away in Vietnam, and so my mom and two sisters raised me.

Football and sports were my life growing up. When I was 10 we moved to Knoxville, and life was great.

Great, that is until the phone rang on my 14th birthday, April 16, 1978. I still remember my mom crying out, "No! No! What's wrong, Gene?" The call was to tell us that my sister had been in a horrible car accident, and soon we were on our way to the University of Tennessee hospital. I remember thinking, "Susan will be all right, just like in the movies." Then the doctor took us aside and showed us some material from Susan's clothes to confirm her identity; he told us that she had died at the scene of the accident. I just sat there, stunned. I remembered how earlier that day Susan had danced and shown off her new dress for the Sigma Chi party that night. She was only 20, my best friend, and my second mom. She had taught me how to play football and baseball. But now she was gone.

Family and friends surrounded us during this tough time. I remember going home the morning Susan died and falling asleep. I awoke later to my father crying out in the next room, "No, God, not my daughter! How could you do this?"

My buddies took care of me, and I got back into school and sports. Ken Sparks, my coach at Farragut High School, eventually invited me to spend the weekend at a Fellowship of Christian Athletes (FCA) annual weekend camp. To make him happy, I said yes. That weekend I accepted Jesus as my personal savior. A couple years ago, my mother showed me my 5th grade yearbook that Susan had written in: "I hope that someday you'll know Jesus Christ as your personal savior as I know him." Susan's wish had come true. I know Susan is in Heaven and I can't wait to dance with her again.

Interestingly, Fellowship of Christian Athletes not only brought me to Jesus, it brought me my wife! After high school I received a scholarship to play football at the University of Tennessee. (After only two years on the team, I suffered a shoulder injury that ended my football dreams.) While a freshman at UT, I was invited to speak at a Farragut High School FCA huddle group. That's when I saw Cathy. She was gorgeous, but way too young – she was only a high school freshman. I would have to wait.

Finally, when I was a college junior and Cathy was a senior in high school, I called and asked her out. She said yes, even though she didn't remember what I looked like (it had been several years). After graduation, Cathy enrolled at UT. We dated for more than three years and in 1989, a week after we both graduated from college, we were married.

Following our honeymoon in Hawaii, we packed our belongings and moved to Melbourne, Florida, for my new career with Harris Corporation. In Melbourne, we attended Palm Bay Christian Church, and I taught the Sunday-morning high school class. Everything was falling into place; our life as a married couple was off to a good start. The only thing left to do was start having kids.

Cathy was ready for children; in fact, she had been ready since she was a little girl. In 1991 Cathy's dream came true when she gave birth to our first child. Casey was so beautiful. She looked like Cathy – dark skin and lovely eyes. I still remember the look on Cathy's face as she held Casey. Cathy was complete. She had her baby and all was well.

Less than two years later, Morgan joined the family. She was incredible, with blond hair and fair skin like me. Okay, I'll admit it. I had wanted a boy, but Morgan took my heart. My boss and mentor, Bill Tankersley, had a saying: "Boys are good, but little girls are special." He was right.

The Moellers were still on cruise control. I had a great job, Cathy was at home with the girls, and we loved our church. Only one thing was missing: Knoxville – our home. Finally, after six-and-a-half years in Melbourne, I got a job in Knoxville in the telecom industry. We were moving home to grandparents (free babysitting), UT football, snow, and trees. Yea!

The joy we anticipated was realized, but not without some bad times between the good. Not long after we moved home, Cathy became pregnant; sadly, the pregnancy ended in a miscarriage. Cathy was devastated. Before long, she was pregnant again, only to be heartbroken nine weeks later when she miscarried again. Finally, several months later, Cathy was pregnant again, but this time nine months passed and we had our third daughter, Kendall. Kendall was gorgeous as well, and I was now happily surrounded by women.

But then there was more bad news. Cathy's father was diagnosed with cancer. Ed drew strength from his faith, though, and he shared with us words that have supported us in difficult times. He saw himself in a "win-win" situation with cancer. "If I die from cancer, I get to meet my Lord. If I survive cancer, I get to stay with Julia and my family. I win either way." And on July 7, 1998, he won!

As time passed, our schedules got busier and busier, and suddenly we found ourselves on a treadmill moving at high speed. We weren't cruisin' anymore – we were just holding on for dear life!

A few months later Cathy asked me if I had ever considered adopting a baby. In fact, she told me, it had been a life-long dream of hers. I was surprised and didn't respond positively at first, but Cathy provided an incentive. "We can get a son for you!"

After much prayer and many financial blessings from God, in January of 2000 I agreed. Eight months later we were on our way to Vladivostok, Russia, to see my son. We named him Luke. He was 14 months old, weighed 14 pounds, and looked just like me. We couldn't take him home yet (it took two trips to adopt in Russia), but I had a son.

Following our second trip to Russia we returned to Knoxville with Luke. My dad (who was the Assistant Athletic Director of the University of Tennessee) had arranged for Smokey, the UT mascot, to be at the airport along with our family, friends, and church family. It was one of the best days of my life. Once again, we were cruisin'.

Our spiritual life, we believed, was strong. We attended church each Sunday, taught Sunday school, tithed – we were doing all the right things for God. Oh sure, we sinned, but we considered ourselves to be good people. I often jokingly tell folks that I even went to Russia to adopt so I could get extra credit with God. (You know us football players; we always need extra credit.) Before long, our faith would be tested to the limit.

Playing outside.
June 2001

Our middle daughter, Morgan, was now 8 years old, attending Concord Christian School, and a very healthy straight A student. At Concord she was everyone's best friend.

Not only was she a fine student, she was a gifted athlete. In soccer, they called her the "Big Boot." She could kick the soccer ball so hard they would let her sit back at mid-field and try to score. I still remember her last big kick in soccer in the spring: she almost scored, and everyone was impressed. Morgan was also an excellent gymnast and had been asked to be on a competitive team. Everywhere she went she was doing cartwheels, round-offs, and round-off back hand-springs.

A gorgeous, loving girl, Morgan was also caring. She would carry her baby brother Luke around on her hip and watch over him constantly. It was almost as if she had given birth to Luke and was his mama. Morgan always wanted to please us and make us happy.

She was the daughter every father dreams about, and she had a special place in my heart. She was my buddy. We went and looked at cars together, we went to Lowe's together, and she drank my Diet Mountain Dew.

Every night at bedtime, Morgan and I would go through a little ritual. First, we'd say our prayers, and then I'd lay down with her. After several minutes, I'd get up and tell Morgan how proud I was of her and how much I loved her. Morgan would respond with, "Daddy, I love you. Daddy, I'm proud of you. Good night." It was music to my ears, and it made me understand a little better how God must feel when we tell Him we love Him.

Going to church.
June 2001

Now it was late 2001, we were cruisin' through life, and life was very good. I remember a moment, though, when I sensed that things were about to change. Cathy and I were leaving the UT campus, where I had just received a letterman's ring from

Coach Fulmer (the head football coach for the University of Tennessee). As I pulled through the traffic light, I said to Cathy, "Things are going so well, I feel like something's going to happen. It just can't keep going so well."

Two weeks later, Morgan was critically ill and in the intensive care unit at Children's Hospital fighting for her life. Suddenly our cruising had stopped and everything was in slow motion.

Morgan (right) and her sister Casey.
Christmas Play 2000

chapter two

THINGS GET BAD: MORGAN *is* DIAGNOSED *with* DIABETES

October 28th started out as a typical Sunday morning in the Moeller household. Chaos reigned. Cathy had gotten up early to get the girls' hair done and their dresses lined up while I wrestled with Luke to get him ready. Luke preferred his pajamas to Sunday clothes, so getting him dressed and ready for church was always interesting.

After church Morgan ran across the parking lot and met me in the youth house, where I had been teaching Sunday school. I got my usual kiss and hug.

To this point, nothing was out of the ordinary; but from here on, nothing was going to be the same. For starters, Papa (my dad) was taking Casey and Morgan to a cheerleading competition at the UT campus. I still remember how excited Morgan was in the van, bouncing up and down on the seat with a huge smile on her face. When the three of them returned home from the competition, the girls were even more excited. Papa had managed to get them some trophies (he was always good at getting stuff for the kids), which they showed off.

Finally, things began to settle down. But as we got ready for dinner, Morgan said she didn't feel well. Cathy had prepared Morgan's favorite dinner, Pizza Rolls, but Morgan didn't feel like eating. She just put her head down on the table and sat there.

Monday would, of course, be a school day, so after dinner it was time for bed. Because she wasn't feeling well, Morgan asked Cathy to lay down with her. This was usually my job, but Morgan wanted Mommy tonight. So Cathy laid down with Morgan, snuggled up close, and rubbed her head. Finally Morgan went to sleep and Cathy got up and left her room.

Cathy and I awoke around 5:30 a.m. to find Morgan standing in our bedroom throwing up. She looked really sick, white as a sheet. I quickly rushed Morgan into the bathroom and started to clean her up. Cathy put Morgan in sweat clothes and they went downstairs where Morgan sat on the couch. Around 8:00 a.m., Cathy called the doctor and took her right in for an exam. I went off to work thinking that Morgan was a little sick but that she'd be fine.

I hadn't been at work long when Cathy called to let me know she was keeping Morgan home for the day; the doctor had said Morgan had a virus. Instead of improving, however, Morgan just kept throwing up and was getting dehydrated. Later that afternoon, Cathy called to tell me that Morgan had gotten much worse – she was lethargic – and that they were going back to the doctor's office.

Another exam and some tests didn't seem to reveal much. A urine sample showed that Morgan had a high ketones level, but that was to be expected because she was so sick. They also tested her blood sugar and for some unexplained reason it came back fine. (We learned later that the machine was not capable of registering such a high blood sugar number!)

It was clear, though, that Morgan was extremely dehydrated. So, with some difficulty (the dehydration was so severe that her veins had collapsed), they started an IV and sent her and Cathy to Children's Hospital to get Morgan hydrated. Apparently, Morgan was barely responding; she never even flinched when they poked her with the IV needle.

About 4:30 in the afternoon Cathy called and told me she was on her way to the hospital with Morgan to get her hydrated. I quickly left work and got to the drop-off area of Children's Hospital before they did. I remember Cathy driving up in the minivan. Next to her, hunched over in the front seat, was Morgan in her blue sweat outfit. She looked very sick.

Cathy found an empty parking space right in front. I opened the door and Morgan put her arms around me as I carried her inside. By this time she was so weak she could no longer walk.

Something else was different about Morgan. She was breathing unbelievably fast. It was as if she had just run a 200-yard dash and couldn't get her breath. She was so exhausted that she just collapsed in my arms. Children's Hospital knew we were coming, and so we spent only a short time in the waiting room before we were taken to her room on the 3rd floor.

The nurses didn't want her to drink since she was still throwing up, but Morgan kept saying "I'm so thirsty" and pleading for a sip of anything. Finally, we got her a sip of water. Soon a nurse came into the room to draw blood. It took her nearly 20 minutes to get the blood since Morgan's veins had collapsed. Finally, the nurse left with the sample and we just sat there talking. By this time they decided Morgan could have something to drink so they gave her a Sprite. I was holding Morgan's hand and Cathy was rubbing Morgan's head. She looked better and was talking a little bit to both of us.

Thirty minutes later, around 7:00 p.m., the nurse came in again for another blood sample. We thought this was odd, but Morgan, a trooper as usual, just gave them her arm and hand and they took more blood. About 15 minutes later Morgan was getting thirsty and asked for something cold, like a Popsicle. Cathy volunteered to find the nurse and the Popsicle.

Cathy was gone for what seemed too long a time, so I went into the hallway to look for her. There she was in the hallway, crying. She motioned for me to come over to her. "Mike, they think Morgan has diabetes!" I was stunned. I didn't know what to say. We cried together and hugged in the hallway.

Then Cathy, with tears still in her eyes, said, "You know, it could be worse. She could have something else, like cancer. We can do this; we can handle this." Cathy was so faithful and brave. I, on the other hand, was devastated.

With that diagnosis, the tone changed. A nurse quickly brought Morgan Diet Sprite and ice chips. Someone had called the Endocrinology Department, and Dr. Nichols was on his way to the hospital. We began making calls to our parents. I remember my mom's reaction. Like me, she was devastated. There was no history of Type 1 diabetes in either of our families. I just remember my mom saying "Mike you're kidding me; you're kidding me." The rest of our family and friends (many from church) soon found out and were on their way to Children's Hospital.

After a short time – it was now around 8:00 p.m. – Dr. Nichols arrived to confirm the bad news. Morgan did have diabetes; her blood sugar was around 600. Morgan also had high ketones (acid in the blood).

Dr. Nichols told us that Morgan would be in the hospital 3 to 4 days. During that time we would learn how to handle diabetes and count carbohydrates. He also told us there was a very small chance of complications setting in during the next 12 hours. This rarely ever happens, he told us, but he wanted to move her to the Intensive Care Unit (ICU) as a precautionary measure. They would be able to watch Morgan more closely there.

As we waited to be moved to ICU, Morgan seemed to be feeling better. I took this opportunity to snuggle up with her in the hospital bed. The bed was not very large and I'm not a small guy. It was pretty tight as I balanced on the edge of the bed with my arms around her. I remember saying to myself, "This may be the last time I get to snuggle with Morgan. I need to remember everything about her and how I feel." At the time it didn't make sense, but I know now that God was preparing me and giving me one more moment to remember.

Around 9:00 we finally got the clearance to go to ICU. I decided I would carry Morgan up to the 5th floor. She was doing a little better and gave me a kiss when I picked her up. So there we were, on our way to ICU to begin our new life with diabetes, we thought. We had listened to Dr. Nichols as he told us about the rare chance of complications, but I had shrugged it off like a one-in-a-million chance of being hit by lightning.

After we got Morgan into ICU and settled, I went outside to the waiting room. By this time my mom, dad, and sister had arrived. We all cried together as I told them what the doctor had said. My sister, Diane, my hero in the hospital, took control. She was once a nurse supervisor in ICU at Children's Hospital. In fact, many of the nurses she had trained and managed were now running the show. Diane got one of the nurses to open up the consulting room just outside of ICU where we quickly set up shop. The room was small (only about 5 x 8 feet) and crowded with four chairs, a small couch, and a couple tables – crammed, but private.

I made my way to the waiting room where friends and some members of our church were waiting. I remember most Janelle Covert standing there crying. I hugged her first. You see, just a couple of months before, Janelle (then 16) was diagnosed with Type 1 diabetes. As we hugged, I told Janelle: "You and Morgan can now be buddies. I need you to help her out." She nodded yes and cried some more.

Before long, I returned to ICU and took over the watch as Cathy went to get our things from the third-floor room. Cathy asked Jill Branson, one of her best friends, to go with her. On the elevator Cathy broke down. "All Morgan ever wanted was to be a mommy, and now she won't be able to have babies." You see, the only things we knew about diabetes were what we had seen on TV. How misinformed we were. Later that night one of the nurses explained more about the disease. She talked about all the moms with diabetes having healthy babies. We were relieved to hear the truth.

We stayed in ICU with Morgan as the staff began the process of getting her hydrated and lowering her blood sugar with insulin. Morgan was resting. Cathy sat beside her bed and held her hand. I sat down beside them, and all was quiet for awhile. There wasn't much to say. I was crying but trying to be strong. Cathy, on the other hand, was the cornerstone. She had on her game face for this new life of diabetes. As she said, "We can handle this; it could be worse."

It was now around midnight, and our friends and family had gone home. Cathy decided she would take the first shift and hang out in ICU with Morgan. Cathy urged me to get some sleep since I would be taking the second shift later that night. I agreed, but first I told her I needed to make some calls. Looking back, somewhere and somehow my priorities were mixed up. Of all things, I went outside to leave a message for my boss and to tell a customer that I wouldn't be able to make a meeting the next day. My daughter was in Intensive Care and I was worried about work! What was I thinking?

After making the calls I went back into ICU and lay down beside Morgan on her bed. She was so beautiful resting there as the nurses worked to get her blood sugar down. It was going well. When I finally left to lie down in the consultation room, Morgan's blood sugar was around 250 and dropping. Everything seemed to be under control. Not a hint of complications; they didn't even cross my mind.

But other thoughts did. I sat in the room for awhile by myself and cried. "How could this be happening? Is this just a dream?" I pinched myself. No, it was real. I prayed that night for God to help Morgan and to help us through this time. I had no idea what was about to take place and how much we were going to need His help.

Around 1:00 or 1:30 a.m., I curled up on the small couch (a very small couch) to try to get some sleep. I remember thinking and worrying. "God, how are we going to do this? My daughter has diabetes. Why? Why is this happening to us?" Finally, I fell asleep as Cathy snuggled with Morgan in ICU. My sleep would be brief, however.

chapter three

THINGS GET WORSE: MORGAN *has* BRAIN DAMAGE

About 2:30 in the morning Cathy took Morgan to the bathroom and put some pajamas on her. Morgan's blood sugar was coming down nicely, and she seemed to be feeling better. Cathy snuggled with her in the ICU bed and rubbed her head as they talked about what was going on and why she was in the hospital. Morgan finally seemed able to relax and peacefully drifted off to sleep. "She looked like an angel," Cathy said.

But the peace that Cathy felt lasted for only a second as she quickly realized that something was terribly wrong. She shook Morgan. No response. She yelled, "Morgan, wake up!" Nothing. By this time the nurses had rushed over to find out what was wrong.

Soon, Cathy burst through the door to the small consulting room in a panic. "Mike, there's something wrong!" I quickly got up and ran into ICU. She looked horrible: her color was gray and her eyes were going in different directions. She looked dead. The nurses (six to eight of them) were scrambling to get new IVs and a catheter into Morgan; others were calling doctors to get instructions. It was controlled chaos and I was helpless. There was Morgan, my little girl, dying in front of me.

I looked at Cathy and she was just standing there stunned and crying, but I know she was praying. We were standing as close as we could to Morgan telling her it was going to be okay and Mommy and Daddy were right here. But Morgan would not respond. The nurses soon asked us to back up so they could work on Morgan. I was so helpless. Morgan was dying; we were losing her. I did the only thing I could. I dropped to my knees and starting begging and pleading with God to save her. "Please God, don't take my Morgan. She can't die." I'll never forget the feeling I had. My heart hurt so badly. It felt like it was going to explode. I don't remember how long I stayed on my knees. Every second felt like an hour, and every minute felt like a day. Time stopped for me.

When I finished praying, I got back to my feet. By this time, the nurses had gotten a medicine called "Mannitol" into Morgan to get her body to release the fluid that was causing her brain to swell. When they had put in the catheter, Morgan's body jerked, and the nurses commented that that was a good sign.

They continued to work on Morgan, getting her ready to go to the 1st floor for an emergency CAT scan to see exactly what was happening with her. I then remembered my sister. She had told me to call her if anything happened, so I grabbed a phone and called, waking Diane from a deep sleep. All I said was, "We're losing Morgan, Diane." She quickly rushed to the hospital.

We walked beside Morgan's bed as they took her down for the CAT scan. By this time they were using a hand bagger to help Morgan breathe. The nurses looked scared. They knew Morgan might not make it. As they were getting ready to move Morgan into the CAT scan, I loudly said, "Morgan!" and she jerked. But it was a different kind of jerk; she stiffened when she moved. You could see concern in the nurses' eyes and in how they looked at each other. Cathy and I felt good that Morgan had responded, but the nurses saw posturing starting, which meant that Morgan's body was dying.

They started the CAT scan and soon ICU's head physician showed up. He asked us to leave the room and wait outside. By this time Diane had arrived and the three of us just stood there waiting. It was now around 3:30 a.m. Fifteen to twenty minutes later the doctor came out of the CAT scan room and told us that he had decided to take over everything for Morgan, and she was now on a ventilator. Suddenly we realized that our one-in-a-million, chance-of-a-lifetime, threatening complication from the onset of diabetes was confirmed. Her brain was swelling uncontrollably, and there was little that could be done to stop it.

I remember Morgan the next time I saw her. She had so many tubes and IVs coming out of her. The ventilator was bad enough, but they had placed in her inner thighs two central lines for her medicines and blood pressure. They had now moved her insulin IV into her ankle. She had a catheter and IVs coming out of her arms and hands. Cathy and I later counted 16 tubes running out of her body. It was overwhelming. I just sobbed every time I looked at my little girl.

Before long, Morgan was back upstairs in ICU. From 4:00 a.m. to 6:00 a.m. was a blur. I don't remember anything. The pain blocked out everything. Around 6:00, we were told that we would be meeting a neurosurgeon, and the doctors wanted to drill a hole in Morgan's skull and place a device to measure her brain pressure. We consented and soon Morgan had a "bolt" placed in her brain – that meant another wire running out of her body. The new monitor showed brain waves and pressure and had a large number on the screen. We were told to watch the number, or ICP (intracranial pressure), which should read between 0-5 for a normal reading. Morgan's was now running 15 and her brain pressure was quickly climbing.

"The next few days will be wait and see," the doctor told us. I didn't realize at the time that what he meant was "wait and see if she'll live." I was thinking, "wait and see that she'll be okay." A few days later we found out that 90 percent of the children with this complication don't survive. And for those who do survive, the outcome is very bad. We also found out that Morgan was only 10 to15 minutes away from her brain completely herniating into the brain stem. If this had happened, Morgan would have died or have been brain dead. I'm thankful I didn't learn these things until later. I don't believe I could have made it through knowing that information.

Now it was 9:00 a.m. and Morgan's brain pressure was still rising into the 20s and 30s (remember that 0-5 is normal). I had left ICU while Cathy stayed with Morgan. Soon after, Cathy came into the consulting room a second time in a panic. "Mike, it's getting bad." We both rushed back into ICU to see a team of doctors and nurses working on Morgan and having a discussion. They looked at us and asked us to stand back. Soon, a nurse came to us and asked us to leave ICU. We knew Morgan's condition was bad, very bad. We could see that the brain pressure reading had now gone over 60 and was still climbing. As Cathy and I walked down the hall holding each other, Cathy looked at me and said, "I know God has a plan, but

His plan really stinks right now. This can't be his plan for Morgan." We just stood there together and cried.

What we did not understand was that God was coming to the rescue. After finding out about Morgan, the staff at Morgan's school decided to have a prayer time for her. It was around 9:15 and Concord Christian School stopped what they were doing and prayed for Morgan. These kids didn't just pray, "God give her strength." They wanted Morgan to be well and back to school playing with them on the playground.

We know that at this same time, Morgan's brain pressure started to come down very quickly. This was unexpected by the doctors and nurses. Within a couple of minutes her pressure reading was in the teens again. Was it the doctors? The drugs they gave her? Prayers from a school and hundreds of kids? We believe that God saw the kids praying, heard their prayers, and then moved in and saved Morgan.

By this time our family, friends, and church family were now showing up to see what they could do. It was comforting to see how many people cared about Morgan and our family. It meant so much that so many people were lifting up Morgan and our family in prayer.

About this time, one of my best friends, Scott Branson, came walking down the hall. Cathy told him, "She may not make it, Scott." He hugged her and then came over to me, gave me a big hug, put his head on my shoulder, and then we cried together. We spoke no words. We just cried. That was exactly what I needed. I didn't need someone to tell me it was going to be okay or that this was God's plan. I just needed someone to cry with me and share my intense pain. Thank you, Scott.

Tuesday felt like an eternity. There was a line of people just standing in the hallway not knowing what to say. Some were bringing food, drinks, and gifts. Someone brought Morgan a praying, tan-colored, stuffed bear that we placed over her bed in ICU. One of Morgan's friends, Gracie, had her mother bring in a CD player and some of her favorite CDs. We treasured this gift. Mrs. Bridges, Morgan's teacher, also brought in another CD with Morgan's favorite song, "Arise my Love," by the group Newsong. But mostly, we just sat there and cried together.

Most of the time Cathy and I were in ICU watching Morgan. We had been given instructions not to talk to her or touch her. They didn't want her brain to have any outside stimulation or excitement. Morgan was in a drug-induced coma, and they wanted us to be as quiet as possible for her. When people would talk around her or there was a loud noise, you could see her pressure reading rise. Her reading was hanging around the 30s most of the day. I must have prayed a thousand times over the next few days for the pressure reading to go down. It was something I could focus on. If it was low, I felt better; if it was high, I felt worse.

Throughout the day, people came up to ICU to check on Morgan. Our three other children were being transported from friends to friends. Cathy was trying to keep their schedules straight while we talked to the kids on the phone to assure them things were going to be okay. The problem was, we didn't know if everything was going to be okay.

Cathy's mother, Julia, moved into our home to keep things as normal as possible. Little did she know she had come to stay for four months!

My dad was at the hospital the entire time. He just sat there in his chair in the consulting room and told me when to eat and when to sit down. I knew that if I needed anything, he would get it. If anything needed doing, he would do it.

On Tuesday night, something else happened that changed my heart forever. A large crowd gathered (not for Morgan) in the hallway. A teenager was dying of leukemia and wasn't expected to make it through the night. As I was walking back and forth between ICU and our little room, I stopped to talk with a couple and asked them if they were part of the family in the hallway. "No," they replied, "we just got here with our son Billy." They looked as scared as I was, and so we kept talking. They had recently moved to Knoxville, and their son, less than a year old, had a horrible disease called Spinal Muscular Atrophy. In ICU, Billy was placed in the bed next to Morgan. Bill and Lisa, Billy's parents, could see how sick Morgan was, but their son was also very sick. We became close friends there. It was like I had someone I could help. I couldn't touch Morgan, but I could help Bill and Lisa with food, blankets, and my cell phone to call their parents. Most of all, I had Billy to pray for every time I passed by his bed. It was something other than Morgan that I could think about for just a second – a momentary escape from our own tragedy.

We knew this was going to be a long night. I was still watching the pressure readings and praying they would stay down. George Clark (our minister) came in with me to ICU to pray for Morgan. We were on our hands and knees in ICU praying. I know that Morgan's appearance was unsettling to George too: the tubes, the pressure gauge, the ventilator were almost more than either of us could take.

After George left we settled in for a long night. Our family journey had taken a sudden turn for the worse. We were in a fierce battle for Morgan's life. I pleaded with God to end the pain and have Morgan wake up the next day. I just sat there in a rocking chair looking at all the monitors. The nurses were great. They would bring me blankets that were heated in the microwave to keep me warm during the night. I spent many hours and days in the rocking chair beside Morgan's bed. I loved the rocking chair. It had been donated by a father in memory of his daughter. But most of all, I loved the scripture on the chair – Psalm 38:14: "God comforts the broken hearted." My heart was broken and I needed comfort. Boy, I needed comfort.

Wednesday finally came. Cathy and I took shifts and I got a couple hours of sleep during the night. We were still running on adrenaline and watching Morgan's brain-pressure monitor. The nurses now knew us well in ICU, and when we rang the buzzer to enter, I just said, "Morgan's dad," and they let us in. I would walk by Billy's bed, pray for him, and then sit down by Morgan. Cathy stayed there pretty much all of the time. She didn't want to leave Morgan's side, and neither did I.

Wednesday was a tough day. It was very loud in ICU with many babies crying and some construction. I remember getting angry at the situation. Morgan needed it to be quiet. You could see her pressure increase as the babies cried. We needed to go someplace else, but where? The hospital was adding some rooms at the end of ICU, but they weren't yet equipped to handle Morgan.

It was then that God moved in again. By Thursday morning, they had a room completely equipped and ready for use. Morgan would be the first child to use the new ICU private room. Thank you, God!

During the day on Wednesday, Morgan was taken care of by an incredible nurse. His name was Bill, and he really took care of Morgan. I remember how organized he was and how he truly cared for Morgan. Somehow, she had touched Bill's heart. He got all of Morgan's IVs and tubes organized, color-coded, and labeled. He next got her into better positions so she would look more "ladylike," as he would say. Bill also had the tough job of placing a tube through Morgan's nose for feeding her vanilla-flavored Pediasure. Bill took care of Morgan a couple more times in ICU, and each time he did something special for her. Other nurses were special as well, but you could tell that Bill had connected with Morgan.

Late Wednesday afternoon the doctors told us that on Thursday they were going to do another CAT scan to see if there was any brain damage. We were excited about this because if the CAT scan was okay, they would begin to wake Morgan, and we could get out of the hospital. At the same time I was nervous. What if the CAT scan is bad? What if Morgan has brain damage? The nurses, my sister, and our pediatrician were all thinking positive. "It will be okay; we think we caught it early." We were very hopeful. I was ready for Morgan to hop up into my lap, give me a kiss, and say, "Daddy, I love you." Oh, how I missed those words. I would have given anything to hear them just one more time. Hopefully, soon, I thought to myself.

After taking shifts throughout the night, Cathy and I started a new day with great hope that the CAT scan would show no brain damage. The thinking of the doctors and nurses was that they had caught the brain swelling early enough to stop any damage.

Around 9:00 o'clock, they started getting Morgan ready for the CAT scan. It would take four or five nurses just to handle all of the IVs and to bag Morgan until they could get her to another ventilator. As they started the CAT scan, they allowed Cathy and me to stay in the room.

A couple minutes later, the doctors and nurses starting viewing the images in a control room. From where Cathy was standing, she couldn't see into the room, but the room had a large window and I could. I can still see their faces. They were crying and shaking their heads. You could see the disappointment in their faces and in their tears. It wasn't good. My heart sank and suddenly my hope turned to fear.

The doctor walked out of the room and came over to us. "Let's go upstairs." That was all he said. His body language told us the rest. It was really bad. No one spoke as we rode the elevator back to ICU. Our doctor led Cathy, Diane, and me into one of the new private rooms to tell us about Morgan's condition. She had significant brain damage (infarqs), and the damage to her brain stem was severe on the left side. I began crying out: "How could this have happened? Just a couple days ago she was running around playing, and now she has brain damage? This is my daughter! This is my little Morgan!"

I was overwhelmed and I dropped to my knees, put my head on Cathy's lap, and cried. Cathy was crying too, but she kept saying, "God has a plan. God has a plan." Cathy truly felt everything was going to work out. I wasn't so sure. For me, this was the worst day of my life. I begged and pleaded, "God, take this burden from me."

Soon Morgan arrived back in ICU, but this time she was placed in the private room, as we had hoped. The rest of Thursday was very, very difficult. All I could think about was Morgan's brain damage. I began having visions of her on a ventilator, sitting in a wheelchair, gazing into space. Our other children would be playing outside, and I'd go up to Morgan every now and then and give her a kiss on the forehead. I'd tell her I love her, but she wouldn't respond. She'd just sit there looking right past me.

As friends and family came to ICU to try to help, we'd tell them about Morgan's condition. Like us, they were stunned and didn't know what to say. They just cried, gave us a hug, and lowered their heads. There was nothing any of us could say.

It was around this time that Cathy and I came up with a goal for Morgan. We decided that Morgan would walk as a bridesmaid in Angela's (Cathy's sister's) June wedding. The goal was crazy, but it was something we could hold onto and hope for. Here we were, fighting for Morgan's life, but somehow and from somewhere, our goal was to see Morgan walking in six months.

Thursday evening found me in ICU rocking in my favorite rocking chair and staring at the pressure reading. All I could think about was Morgan's brain damage and the permanency of her condition.

At about 9 p.m., I thought I ought to check on Cathy. She had gone to the small consultation room to be by herself. When I arrived, I found the door to the room closed and I could hear music playing inside. I opened the door and there was Cathy, reading the Bible, worshiping and praising God, and smiling. I sat down beside her and we began worshiping God in prayer and song. The Holy Spirit was there with us. I could feel His presence. Then, suddenly I felt my heart lighten and joy come over me like never before. God had not forsaken us. He now had us, His children, in His hands and was taking our burdens as He promised. But He didn't take them by force. It was only when we truly handed them to Him that he took them from us. As we worshiped together we lifted our hands to God and gave Morgan back to him. There in our small room Cathy and I prayed "Lord, we give you Morgan. She's yours. You love her more than we do and want the best for her. We thank you for eight wonderful years with her." We were ready to follow God's plan for Morgan whatever that might be. If He wanted to take Morgan now, we were okay with that. It was like the weight of the world drifted away. We handed everything over to God that night as the Scripture tells us in 1 Peter 5:7: "Cast all your anxiety on Him because He cares for you."

chapter four

THINGS GET AWFUL: MORGAN *won't* WAKE UP

I t was now Friday morning, November 2nd. Morgan had a better night's sleep since it was very quiet in the room, and her pressure readings were now in the teens to 20s. We still couldn't touch her or talk to her. So, I started smelling Morgan. Yes, I had gone crazy, but I distinctly remember smelling her knee every time I came into the room and whenever I left. It comforted me so much just to be able to smell her.

Morgan was never alone in the room. We wanted someone to be there just in case she woke up. That was what we told ourselves, but really, we just needed to be there by her. It's hard to describe this feeling, but parents with critically ill children will understand it.

While Morgan was fighting her illness, Cathy's sister Angela was on a mission trip in Russia. We had been able to reach her and let her know of Morgan's struggle. During one of the revivals there, Angela told them about Morgan. More than 3,000 people in Russia prayed for Morgan that night! If when two or more are gathered in the name of Jesus there is power, how much power must there be when 3,000 are praying?

We also had several of our friends tell us that they were praying on their knees and were up late every night praying for Morgan. Many told us, "I've never prayed so hard and been on my knees so long as I have for Morgan." One of Cathy's best friends, Janette Shofner, prayed for Morgan at every red light when she was in the car. She and her children do that to this day. We were all being continually covered in prayer. Thank you to all who have been so faithful. You will never know the comfort it brought our entire family.

Someone brought Casey and Kendall to the hospital so we could see them. Kendall didn't really understand what was happening, but Casey was heartbroken. Her best buddy was gone and she was scared, so we decided to take Casey in to see Morgan.

We tried to prepare her, but nothing can prepare you for seeing someone as critically sick as Morgan was. The nurses had us go through the back door, because children were not allowed in ICU. I think we just wanted to make sure Casey got to see her sister one more time, just in case she didn't survive. Casey was so brave; she just walked right in. With tears in her eyes, she said, "Okay, now we can go." Later, she told us she thought Morgan was dead and no one was telling her the truth. She just needed confirmation and now she could go on.

Late Friday morning the doctors asked us to meet with them in ICU so they could tell us their plans for Morgan during the weekend. On Saturday, they were going to take out the bolt and begin waking her up. This would be done by slowly taking her off the medication that kept her in a drug-induced coma. I remember the doctor saying, "We think she's going to survive." I almost fell out of my chair. I really hadn't understood how sick Morgan was and that 90 percent of children who have diabetic ketoacidosis (DKA) with cerebral edema do not survive. When that became clear to me, I was excited and relieved. I just wanted to hear the words, "Daddy, I love you." Oh, what I would have paid right then to hear those words just one more time.

Morgan was just like my sister Susan; in fact, Morgan looked very much like Susan and had the same personality. And just as I had lost Susan, I feared that I might lose my Morgan as well. Several years after my sister had died, memories of the little things that Susan did for me were fading. I've always regretted that I hadn't written down some of the little things she did to help me. So, a couple weeks after Morgan got sick and with her future in doubt, I wrote down a list, which I call "Memories of Morgan." I've included part of the list below so you will know Morgan better.

- Last big soccer kick from midfield
- Running pass patterns (the curl)
- How fast she can run
- Cartwheels, one- and two-handed
- Go Bananas cheer
- Sign language to song with Cathy
- Hug on paddle boat from behind and telling me she loves me
- Every night "I love you daddy. I'm proud of you daddy. Good night." Then my goodnight kiss
- Swimming in the lake

- Her laugh and giggle
- Her memory – always remembers
- Coming to find me after church in the youth house
- Putting Luke on her hip, while pushing her hip out
- "Daddy, when are you coming home?"
- Rubbing my arm
- Snuggling on the couch
- Her prayer, "Thank you for my house, my food and our money."
- Her great build – how good she looked in a long, straight dress
- Riding the bike round and round
- Lying in front of the TV with her feet on the entertainment center
- How she walked – short, fast steps
- Hanging onto the basketball-goal rim

The rest of Friday was filled with anticipation and much prayer. I was on my knees a lot praying to God that Morgan would come off the ventilator and wake up. During the afternoon, Scott Branson was able to come in and see Morgan. Only family members and George, our minister, had seen Morgan so far. I think what Scott saw stunned him. Morgan and Scott had a bond that was hard to describe. Scott has three great boys, but Morgan had stolen his heart. Here was "his little girl" on a ventilator and with 16 tubes in her. He broke down in tears. But there, in Morgan's room, Scott shared my pain as another father. It was what I needed just then.

Scott also said something beautiful to me that I'd like to share. He said, "Mike, ministers and missionaries spend their entire life working for the Lord to change the lives of others. Yet, here's a little girl who hasn't spoken a word and is changing people's hearts. Isn't God a mystery?"

Saturday arrived. The neurosurgeon took the bolt out early in the morning and started reducing Morgan's medications to wake her up. Cathy was worried (mostly kidding) that they had shaved a hole for the bolt and ruined Morgan's hair. We figured Morgan could wear a baseball cap for a while.

Around noon Morgan opened her eyes just a little. We asked her to move her fingers and legs. They moved ever so slightly, but they moved. I remember how excited I was. I skipped through ICU as I ran out the door to call my mom and dad. "Mom, Dad, she's opening her eyes! She moved her legs and fingers!" I quickly walked back into ICU, and we kept asking Morgan to move her fingers. They barely moved but it was glorious! We spent the day so excited.

Soon Morgan began gagging on the ventilator; this was expected and a good sign. The hope was that we could take her off the ventilator on Sunday. She slept most of the rest of the day, and we looked toward Sunday with anticipation. It promised to be a big day. I was already imagining Morgan off the ventilator, sitting in my lap giving me hugs." I could hardly wait for tomorrow!

On Sunday, it was time to try to take Morgan off the ventilator. She was now gagging on it fairly often. Because the area in her brain stem that controlled breathing was so severely damaged, there was uncertainty whether Morgan would be able to breathe on her own. The staff asked us to leave as they took it out.

When we returned, Morgan was breathing on her own. They continued to wean her from the morphine and drugs that put her to sleep.

As the day passed, we waited and waited for Morgan to wake up. We were now talking to her, saying her name and asking her to respond. She would ever so slightly open her eyes, but that was all. We continued to wait and worry. Diane reassured us, though, reminding us that it would take a little while for the drugs to wear off. So we waited.

By Sunday afternoon Morgan was still just sleeping. She was not responding. The doctors were puzzled and becoming concerned, and I had reached an emotional low again. I couldn't stand by and watch, so I left Morgan's room and ICU. As I was leaving ICU, I ran into a friend – Heath – and his wife. Between sobs I looked at Heath and said, "Morgan won't wake up." They didn't know what to say. What could they say?

I went into the small consultation room, sat with my head in my hands, and cried. Many people from church were in the room and in the hallway. It was Sunday afternoon and they had come to visit after church. As I wept I heard them say, "It'll be okay, Mike. God has a plan" or "Morgan is young and kids are resilient." Their words were well meant, but they were empty. There was no comfort in them.

Then Scott showed up again. He just grabbed hold of me, there on the floor, and we cried together. He didn't say anything. That was all I needed. At that moment words meant nothing; sharing my pain and agony meant everything.

The next few days were a blur. The doctors decided to do an MRI on Morgan to get a more complete look at the damage. She continued to sleep almost all of the time, and her arms and legs were straight and tight as a board. Her toes were pointed like a ballerina, and her knees were locked tight. We continued to hope and wait for the drugs to wear off, but it was becoming apparent that damage had occurred in a key area of her brain stem and she couldn't wake up. You see, the brain stem is critical. Everything that controls the body's functions, including consciousness and breathing, runs through it.

About this time God sent a young man to relieve some of the pressure. Jared Ross was a student at UT, and he and I went jogging together a couple times. We'd just run and then hang out together for awhile. Equally important, Jared would sit for hours with my dad in the consultation room outside of ICU. He and Dad became close friends and kept each other company while Cathy and I were focused on Morgan.

On Monday night, as I was leaving ICU, I met Craig Covert in the hallway. (If you recall, Craig's daughter Janelle had been diagnosed with juvenile diabetes a couple months earlier.) We decided to go outside for a walk. We didn't talk much at first – we just walked. Eventually we started talking about diabetes and about Craig's friend who has the disease. Then we got to the heart of the matter, sharing how our dreams and hopes for our daughters were being changed. We had something in common.

Without paying much attention to where we were or where we were going, we found our way to an intersection in a residential area. As we stopped at the corner, Craig asked me if I wanted to pray. I said I did, and right there on the corner of Clinch and 22nd Avenue we both got on our knees and prayed.

There we were on the sidewalk right beside the street with a steady stream of cars coming over the hill. It didn't matter; we prayed anyway. I can only imagine what those drivers and passengers must have thought seeing two men on their knees, heads on each others' shoulders in prayer in the middle of the night.

And then something amazing happened. As we finished praying, an older model car came over the hill and stopped right beside us. A woman rolled down her window and asked, "Are you guys praying?" We nodded yes. Then she asked, "Can I pray with you? I'm on my way to the emergency room with my son, but I saw you praying and wanted to stop." I walked over to her car and told her about Morgan and put my hand through the passenger window. She grabbed my hand and started praying for Morgan.

As she finished, I thanked her and she drove up the hill towards the emergency room. Craig and I started walking again, and then what had just happened hit us. A mother going to the emergency room with a child stops and prays with two men who were on their knees at night praying on a street corner. "Are you kidding me?" Craig asked. I believe with all my heart that I met an angel that night, an angel sent from God to touch me, to reassure me. Right there, God let me know He was still in control.

During the day, Cathy and I began taking walks together just to get out of the hospital. On one of our walks – about the same place I had met "the angel" – we sat and talked. We talked about how thankful we were that Morgan had been baptized earlier that year. It meant a lot to us that she was baptized. We weren't concerned that she wouldn't have gone to Heaven if she died; it was more than that. We were thankful that she had openly confessed that Jesus Christ was her Lord and Savior. She had asked to be baptized. The church leadership was concerned that she was only 8, but Morgan loved the Lord and knew she was a sinner and needed a savior. Little did we know that this shy little girl was going to be used in such a powerful way for His glory.

Monday night I decided to get in bed with Morgan to hold her. It was a tight fit and I had to balance on the edge of the bed with the side rail in my back. But it was worth it. I finally had my arm around Morgan and was holding her and telling her I loved her. We were telling Morgan constantly that we were there and that we loved her.

Later that night, Morgan started moaning and crying out. I tried to calm her the best I could, but Morgan couldn't control the moaning and crying. I don't know if she heard me, but she didn't respond. After a couple hours, her crying started wearing on me. "Morgan, Daddy is here. Stop crying," I begged. I was tired and began getting frustrated, even angry, with Morgan. The nurse gave her something to knock her out, and finally she rested.

It was then that my heart sank as I realized that I had gotten angry with Morgan. I asked Morgan to forgive me and asked God for His forgiveness. I was so ashamed. But I was thankful it was over. At least I thought it was over.

The next day Morgan was moaning and crying out like the night before. Her hands, arms, and legs started moving uncontrollably. Morgan's body was becoming contorted and her hands were curled up. We asked the nurses and doctors what was happening. They said the moaning and crying would last a couple days to a couple weeks. My sister called it "neuro crying." It was horrible. Morgan's body was rigid and became distorted. She started looking different. The seriousness of her brain injury was now becoming visibly apparent to us.

Wednesday came and it was time for another MRI. It took fewer nurses this time since Morgan was not on the ventilator and had only a few IVs going. But her arms and legs were moving around uncontrollably, and her eyes were shut. The nurse brought a drug to sedate Morgan during the MRI, but she continued to move out of control. An increased dosage finally got the motion calmed down.

The MRI clearly showed the extent of the brain damage. Though the MRI confirmed the results of the CAT scan, the doctors were still hopeful that Morgan would wake up in a couple days.

It was time to move Morgan to the 2nd floor of the hospital. We had been in ICU for 9 days, and we were ready to move to a private room. As we were moving Morgan's things, I saw my dad sitting in our small consultation room as he had been for the past 9 days. He had left only to get us some food or check on things at work for a few minutes. We sat together and started talking pretty frankly about Morgan, acknowledging that she might never wake up again and if she did, she might exist only as a vegetable.

I then asked my dad about Susan, my sister who had been killed in a car accident 23 years before. "Dad, would you want Susan to be alive if she was like Morgan?" I asked. He didn't hesitate a moment. "Yes, Son, I'd take Susan any way I could have her."

Then Dad told me a story. It was a couple years after Susan had died. He was working in the woods cutting down some trees and clearing underbrush when he realized that sometime during the day he had lost his work keys. There were 20 to 30 keys that he used at his work to open doors to buildings, the stadium, etc. After looking for several hours, he panicked. Dad prayed to God to help him find the keys. Just then a gust of wind blew and leaves started going everywhere. He looked down at his feet, and there were his keys. He told me that on that day, he had felt Susan's touch to help him find the keys. We cried together like never before. It's a time with my dad I'll never forget.

chapter five

OUR NEW LIFE BEGINS: MORGAN *is* UNRESPONSIVE

By late Wednesday afternoon we had moved to the 2nd floor of Children's Hospital. It was wonderful to be out of ICU and in our own room with two beds and a couple of chairs. We were able to move around a little more, and there was room for the cards, flowers, stuffed animals, and food baskets that had been delivered. Cathy put up the posters (10 large ones) that had been sent by classes at Morgan's school. Some of the posters had pictures of her friends accompanied by "Get Well Soon" and "We're praying for you" messages. The nurses commented how much her friends must love Morgan. In addition to the posters, many more cards and pictures were soon taped to the wall. Cathy even took Casey out of school for a day to help her decorate and to spend a little time together.

By now, so many people knew about Morgan and wanted to help that we were being overwhelmed with calls asking about her condition. Ron Bull, our youth minister, came up with a great idea: The church set up a telephone voice mailbox that I would update daily with a report on Morgan and a prayer request. This provided an excellent way for people to keep up-to-date on Morgan's condition. We later found out that individuals would call the number many times each day. Most called from the Knoxville area, but some would call from out of state; other friends and well-wishers would even call from outside the country just to check on Morgan.

Wednesday night came and we were still waiting for Morgan to wake up and respond. . . . Nothing. She neither woke nor responded.

Thursday morning we awoke hoping for a better day. But Morgan just kept sleeping, and sleeping, and sleeping. She opened her eyes only 1 to 2 hours each day. But when her eyes were open, she didn't respond. The doctors were very concerned about her vision. They told us to be prepared for Morgan to be blind.

One of the hardest things was holding Morgan's hand and talking to her with no response in return. She didn't even seem to know we were there. Cathy and I began praying that God would take hold of her spirit and tell her we loved her. We asked Him to take her spirit away from the hospital to a fun place while her body was suffering. We wanted her spirit to be free from the pain of her body. For me it was a way to say, "Morgan, I can't hold your hand and comfort you, but God will hold your spirit and take care of you."

During this time Morgan wouldn't go the bathroom in the diaper provided by the nurses. So Cathy decided we should take her to the bathroom. It was very difficult. Morgan's eyes were barely open, and she had the feeding tube in her nose and a couple of

IVs. She was like a limp rag. The physical work of moving her was strangely comical, but the sobering truth is that it was very sad. We would sit her on the toilet and hold her up. Cathy would tell Morgan it was okay to go to the bathroom, and then Morgan would go. This gave us hope. We knew there was a little bit of Morgan in there. But my heart wanted more, much more.

The therapist came on Thursday and worked with Morgan for several minutes to try to get her to wake up. No luck. So, she'd leave saying, "I'll be back when she's more awake." Later, the therapist would return and start again, but Morgan still wouldn't respond. Next, her neurologist arrived. I wasn't in the room, but Cathy was. He looked at Morgan and said, "Isn't she awake yet?" He thought for a minute and then said out loud: "She may never wake up." Someone had actually said out loud the very thing we had no desire to hear. In spite of those words, we had faith that God would not leave Morgan like this, and we continued to pray for a miracle.

On Friday, the therapist rolled a wheelchair into Morgan's room. It was big and heavy, but we needed to begin getting Morgan accustomed to it. With much time and hard work we got Morgan into the chair. It had a head support, a necessary feature since Morgan wasn't able to hold her head up. The chair also tilted backwards and had arm and leg supports. As we lifted Morgan into the chair, she remained motionless and unresponsive.

Once we had her situated, we set out on a little walk around the 2nd floor. Despite all the motion and the activity around her, Morgan just stared into space. My nightmare was coming true. It was like the image I had seen in my mind in ICU the week before. Morgan's eyes opened only slightly (maybe 10 percent) as she looked past us.

After a couple trips around the floor, my dad took over as motive power. I can still see him today wheeling Morgan around, stopping to look out the window and at different pictures on the walls. He would talk and sing to her as though no one else were around. While they were making the rounds, my dad's best friend, John Michels, showed up at Morgan's room. We talked for a couple minutes before Dad and Morgan came around the corner. When John spotted Morgan his face dropped, and he began to cry. It was too much for him to handle. He continued to cry as he embraced Dad.

Over the next few days, Morgan remained unresponsive. Nevertheless, the doctors and nurses wanted us to try to feed Morgan through her mouth. What a mess! Morgan didn't really chew, but she was able to swallow. We tried yogurt, mashed potatoes, anything soft. Morgan could get a little food down, but it would take 5 to 10 minutes just to get a spoonful into her. We kept trying, though, because the alternative was for Morgan to have a permanent feeding tube placed into her stomach. I didn't want this. Cathy and I were determined to get Morgan eating over the next week. But God had other plans.

Late Friday, a new therapist came in to try to wake Morgan. She wouldn't respond, but this therapist was determined. She sat on the bed with Morgan and rocked back and forth ("big swings" she called them). After doing this for 20 minutes Morgan seemed to hold her eyes open just a little. By then, Scott had showed up, and the therapist asked both of us to help. Then about 15 minutes later, Morgan moved her left leg ever so slightly. You could hardly see it, but it happened. We celebrated! It was a great victory. My heart was filled with joy. But I wasn't satisfied. I then began asking God, "Just let her do something a little new each day, Father. This will give me hope. Please, just a little each day." This was the daily bread I needed to keep going.

My dad had brought a UT cheerleader video to the hospital, and we had some family videos of the kids when they were little, so after the big event we started watching them. Morgan kept her eyes cracked open and watched. And then it happened. As we were sitting in the room talking and eating dinner watching a family video of the kids playing in the snow, Morgan made a sound (laughed out loud for one second). We were all surprised. But that was it. Morgan didn't respond again or smile. But it was okay. What an incredible moment. First Morgan had moved her leg, and now she had laughed out loud. I must have thanked God a hundred times that night.

Soon we fell into something of a routine. One of us would sleep on the bed and the other in a chair next to Morgan's bed. When she would cry out, whoever was in the chair next to her bed would comfort her and tell her we were there. We took two-hour shifts going back and forth between the bed and the chair. In the late evenings from 9:00 to 11:00, Cathy and I would read the Bible, pray, and read cards sent to Morgan and to us. It was amazing how God would put the scriptures we needed to read in the cards we opened. Of course, this wasn't happening by coincidence – it was one way God spoke to us every night.

After a week of this routine, Cathy began staying at home during the night so that our other children could get their mommy back. I would sleep in Morgan's room at the hospital. When Cathy returned around 7:00 the next morning, I would take a shower and head to work. Then I would return to the hospital around 2:00 p.m. to begin the cycle again.

"Work?" you may ask. The fact is, now and then I simply needed to get away a little, and work helped. Maybe "work" isn't the right word. I would go to my office, go through some e-mails, and then just sit in my office and cry. It was all I could do. Thankfully, I had several brothers and sisters in Christ who would take on some of my workload. One time, Chuck Spicka, an employee, came into my office to check on me and ended up crying with me. That's all we did for half an hour. When we were done crying, Chuck prayed for Morgan and me.

But then he said something interesting. "Mike, I can't explain this, but I know Morgan is going to be all right." He wasn't saying it just to make me feel better. He really believed it and said it with conviction. I held onto his words like a life jacket. I wanted Morgan to be okay so badly I would have given every penny I had for that to happen.

While I was at work, Cathy spent the day bathing Morgan, fixing her hair (trying to find styles that would cover her bald spot where they had shaved her head), and doing her nails. The two of them listened to music, and Cathy read out of Proverbs. When Morgan got agitated, Cathy would climb into bed with her to hold her, talk to her, tell her stories, and read to her until she calmed down. Sometimes, this would take more than an hour, and after sitting this long with Morgan leaning against you, your legs and rear end would fall asleep. During these first couple weeks, there was never another response, controlled movement, or recognition by Morgan of any kind.

It was around this time that Love 89, a Christian radio station, began doing a "Morgan update" every morning around 9:00. Someone had called Jason McKay, the DJ, and told him about Morgan. Her story touched his heart. So every morning, he called my voice-mail hot line to get an update and the prayer request for Morgan. We listened to the station several times and were amazed: Thousand of listeners were praying for my daughter!

As for Cathy and me, we were constantly on our knees in prayer. We were praying for a miracle. As I prayed on my knees, my heart would soar and the burdens would lift. The time I spent on my knees was the only time I felt okay – not good or bad, just okay. Cathy felt the same way, and we eventually started calling this our "sanctuary." On our knees we found a place where God comforted us. Yes, I knew He was comforting me all the time, but there was something special about being on our knees.

During the first weekend after leaving ICU, Cathy decided that Morgan's hair needed to be washed. But how? One night, Karen Herbstritt, a friend and head nurse at the hospital, showed us what needed to be done. It was hilarious and took all three of us to get it done. Karen set a trash can next to the bed, and we held Morgan's head over the trash can. Then Karen poured buckets of water over Morgan's head and shampooed her hair. It worked, but what a mess! After that, every other day Morgan was honored to receive a special trash-can hair treatment with the works. We used humor to get through some of our toughest challenges. Thank you, God, for laughter.

On Monday, the hospital performed a swallow test on Morgan. It was successful, so now our goal was to get Morgan eating in a week, the deadline for making a decision on a feeding tube. As we went through the week, we started getting some semblance of routine back. Cathy was at home at night with the kids, and her mother took care of them during the day. I had the night shift and would go to work 2 to 4 hours each day. Morgan was still not responding. My dad came to the hospital all the time and brought food donated by the UT athletic department. By this time, I had lost 15 pounds. All the stress had taken away my appetite. Cathy had lost a lot of weight as well. (But that's all I'll say; she'd get mad if I shared any more information on this subject.)

While all this was going on, the doctors kept trying different drugs to stimulate Morgan so she'd wake up, but nothing worked. The doctors were puzzled and began preparing us for the future they foresaw. For one thing, we needed to begin thinking about a rehab center for Morgan. Our options were Patricia Neal (an adult rehab center), a rehab center in Atlanta, and another center in Nashville. The doctors told us that "most of the recovery would occur in the first six months, at which time it would slow down but continue for another six months. After the first year, there would be very little change."

Hearing this, I thought to myself, "Six months? We've been in here only two weeks and it feels like two years!" I couldn't imagine how we were going to make it another day, much less six months. We were in the survival mode, just trying to make it through the next hour. We had lost track of everything in the world around us. Nothing else mattered. I thought about nothing except Morgan and my family.

During that week we decided to allow the kids to come to the hospital to see Morgan. We knew it would be loud and maybe, just maybe, this would wake Morgan a little. Casey had seen Morgan the week before in ICU and seemed to handle it well. You see, Casey and Morgan were best friends. So, not only had Casey lost her sister, she had also lost her best friend. Casey was very brave and optimistic and told Morgan it was going to be okay. As Kendall came into the room, you could see the shock on her face. She was only 4 years old, and she was stunned. Morgan and Kendall shared a room together at home. Morgan always took care of her little sister Kendall. They played dolls together every day. Suddenly, for Kendall reality set in. Morgan was just lying there doing nothing. Then there was Luke. He was just looking at all the hospital stuff in the room. Thankfully, Luke was too young and too busy doing other things to understand what was happening.

We continued to take Morgan for walks on the second floor every day. On one occasion we asked the nurses if we could take her to the first floor into an open courtyard for some fresh air. The nurses agreed, and we headed with Morgan, unresponsive and gazing, down the elevator. I remember how people looked at her. I knew the look. I had been the same way when I saw someone in Morgan's condition. But this time, it was my daughter. You get feelings of anger as they stare or pretend that you don't exist. But then you realize that they don't understand or know how to deal with the issue.

When we had made our way into the courtyard, Cathy and I sat down in front of Morgan and talked. We asked her – then begged her – to move just her toe or finger. No response. She just sat there. "Please Morgan, move your leg." I watched her leg like a hawk watching a mouse in a field, but her leg didn't move. We then asked Morgan to blink. "Come on, Morgan," we pleaded. "Blink once for yes and twice for no." We were trying to somehow communicate with her. But we got only a blank stare from Morgan, as she looked right past us.

It was here I began to realize that my daughter might never again look me in the eyes. Oh, how I longed for her to look at me. Again, I felt so empty inside. It was the worst of times sitting in the courtyard. Our future seemed to be coming into focus, and it was not what we wanted.

After awhile, we headed into the gift shop. Since Morgan's wheelchair was so big, we bumped into all the walls and racks. We showed Morgan cards, stuffed animals, and other gifts to get a response. Nothing helped. As we were leaving I picked up an elf hat with big ears. I put it on my head and looked at Morgan. Suddenly she smiled, and then she laughed out loud for few seconds. Yay! We were thrilled. I put on other hats, but Morgan didn't respond. It wasn't much, but it was what I needed that day. My daily bread was a laugh.

Morgan still had the feeding tube running through her nose. She was being fed, very slowly, vanilla-flavored Pediasure via a machine. It seemed like Morgan was always getting fed because it would take the machine an hour to feed her. With her snacks and major meals, the machine seemed to never stop.

After a couple weeks of receiving only Pediasure, Morgan began smelling like vanilla. Everything smelled like vanilla. We asked if they had chocolate or strawberry or anything else. Only vanilla for Morgan. I then started calling her "My Vanilla Girl."

One day, Cathy convinced me that I needed to go home and spend the night with the kids. I agreed, and as I drove home, I remembered my anger and asked "God, why me? Why our family?" I looked at other people driving and wished I could be like them. My anger grew as I drove the next 5 miles. I began yelling, screaming, and beating on the steering wheel.

Then, suddenly I realized what I was doing. I felt so guilty that I had yelled at God. I had had my "Job moment." Who was I to be yelling at and questioning God? He loves Morgan more than I do. I begged for His forgiveness. A peace came over me, but how long was it going to last?

As I arrived at home, the kids were very excited. We immediately went into the playroom and started to wrestle. But something was wrong. There was no Morgan. It felt so weird. We played a little while longer, but I finally had to stop. I went into our bedroom, closed the door, and began weeping uncontrollably on the bed. "I've lost my daughter, my Morgan." My heart hurt so bad it felt like it was going to explode. What were we going to do?

In fact, very soon we were again asking ourselves that question. We needed to determine where Morgan's rehabilitation would occur. Cathy and I quickly decided not to split the family again by taking Morgan out of state since one of us (probably Cathy) would have to stay with her in the rehab center for the next few months. That left us two choices: Patricia Neal, a full-time rehab center mainly for adults; or East Tennessee Children's Rehabilitation Center (Children's Corner), an outpatient rehab center for younger children.

On Thursday we prayed that God would make the answer clear, and we took a tour of both facilities. Children's Corner was our choice and Cathy and I were excited. But doctors, counselors, and nurses began warning us not to do this. "Morgan needs full-time care, and you can't take care of her in this condition." But Cathy was determined not to break up our family any more than it already was, and we decided, against professional opinion, to use Children's Corner.

With that decision behind us, we felt we could focus on Morgan and the feeding-tube issue. But then on Friday we received word that our insurance company would pay only for a full-time rehab center (Patricia Neal) and would not cover the cost were we to use an outpatient center, even though it would be much less expensive for them in the long run. But Cathy remained calm and told everyone, "We know where Morgan is supposed to go. It's Children's Corner and God will provide. He'll find a way. He'll make it clear." The nurses and social workers told us "You guys are too nice. You need to go to the newspapers and TV and make this a big deal." But Cathy was firm. "No, we're not going to do that. God is going to provide."

As I talked to Cathy about the insurance over the weekend, she told me there was no option. If the insurance wouldn't pay for it, we'd figure out how to pay for it ourselves. At more than $3000 a week, it was overwhelming. I got angry and started calling everyone I knew – doctors and even our congressman, Jimmy Duncan. Our choice seemed so logical. It was cheaper for the insurance company to do it our way, but they wouldn't listen.

After work on Monday afternoon I arrived at the hospital. Cathy had a big grin on her face. "Guess what," she said. "The insurance company has approved Children's Corner as a special exception." God had come to the rescue! We soon found out that our pediatrician had called the insurance company and asked to talk to a physician to ask for an exception. On that Monday, the usual insurance physician wasn't working. The fill-in physician listened to our pediatrician and said, "I have five children, and one has a disability. This family needs to stay together, so I'll approve your request. This isn't our policy, but I'll personally handle getting the bills paid for you."

As the weekend came to an end, we were running out of time for getting Morgan to eat. If she wasn't eating by Monday, a feeding tube would need to be placed in her stomach. I quickly got onto the voice-mail hotline and made a plea for prayers that Morgan would begin eating and not need a feeding tube.

As the end of the weekend approached, Morgan was still not eating, so the decision was made for her. She'd need to have the feeding-tube operation. I wasn't happy about it, but we had no choice if we wanted to leave the hospital. For me, it was like giving up.

On Monday, Morgan had the operation. Basically, a feeding tube is a hollow tube that leads into your stomach. On the outside of the skin is a small button-like piece of plastic to which a tube would be hooked for feeding. All went well, but as they brought Morgan back to her room, she had changed. Her body was no longer straight as a board and tight. She was now curled up into a ball like a baby. I figured her stomach hurt from the operation and that she would be okay in a couple days. But Morgan didn't straighten out; she remained curled up in a ball. Her right arm was now pointed behind her, and her hands were clenched in a tight fist. She was moaning and crying more.

Thanksgiving was here and we were getting anxious to leave the hospital and go home. Our minister was up for a visit, some prayer, and a little encouragement. As he got up to leave, I volunteered to walk with him to the exit. I wanted to ask a simple question: "George, define for me what it means when people say, 'God will help you get through this.' " I wanted to understand what this meant. Did it mean that in six months, if I were still alive, God had helped me through this?

Right then we walked out the back door of the hospital, and there before me was a hearse. God answered my question. He showed me how it could have been and that I needed to be thankful for what I have.

chapter six

OUR DARKEST DAYS: WE TAKE MORGAN HOME *for* OUR NEW LIFE

It was the Saturday following Thanksgiving. Morgan had spent almost a month in the hospital, but now she was going home. We packed up all our things and got Morgan ready to leave. By now we had been trained on her diabetes treatment (giving shots, taking blood tests, counting carbohydrates), knew how to feed Morgan through her feeding tube, and had been taught how to work all kinds of machines. We were equipped with a Pulsox machine, a suction machine . . . you name it and we had it.

We also had mixed emotions. Oh, of course we were thankful and joyous that we were taking Morgan home, that we'd be putting our family back together, and that we were leaving the hospital.

However, we were also nervous and sad that we were leaving with a daughter who was different from the one we had arrived with a month earlier.

We were starting a new chapter in our journey of life, and though we didn't know it, the story line was going in a direction different from the one we imagined. Our life had been forever changed.

As we left, the nurses gave us hugs and wished us well. You could see in their eyes that they knew we were in for hard times. As we were leaving, Jackie Cook, one of Morgan's nurses took a photo of Morgan. She looks as though she was asleep or blinking, but Morgan was awake. That was all the farther she could open her eyes.

*Leaving the hospital to go home.
Morgan is unresponsive.*

Late November 2001

We put Morgan into a large car seat made specifically for a young adult. It didn't work very well, but we had to have something since Morgan couldn't support herself. I crammed the very heavy and large wheelchair in the back of our minivan, and off we went. When we were about halfway home Morgan started crying (screaming is probably more like it) very loud. Just imagine an 8-year-old child screaming as though she had just hurt her leg in a bad bicycle accident. We tried to calm her but she simply got louder and louder and louder! She cried non-stop the rest of the way home.

We hoped Morgan would quit crying when we got home, but she didn't – couldn't – stop. Her illness had taken her into a new, more terrible, phase. No longer was she moaning or crying softly. Now she cried as if she were terrified. She didn't stop – day or night.

When we arrived home, Scott was putting the finishing touches on a door and temporary wall in our dining room. This was Morgan's new room. It was furnished with a hospital bed and a couch that folded out into a small bed. We had all of her medications (muscle relaxer, sleep medicine, insulin for the diabetes, and a variety of other medicines) on a countertop in the kitchen. It looked like a drugstore. Julia, Cathy's mother, who had moved in to help with the other kids, was now going to help us with Morgan as well. She was an incredible blessing for us.

It was good to be home, but all we could hear was Morgan screaming in the dining room, yelling at the top of her lungs. Nothing would comfort her, but we tried anyway. Soon, the other kids began to be affected by it. They would walk around with their hands over their ears and ask, "Mommy, why won't she stop screaming?" We all wanted to help her out, but there seemed to be nothing we could do. She was just screaming. Our oldest daughter, Casey, read books to her to no avail. Kendall helped take care of Morgan and watched movies in bed with her. We tried everything we could think of to calm her down, but nothing worked. We all missed the Morgan we used to know.

Our refrigerator was full of ham, chicken, casseroles, and desserts delivered to us by friends and other supporters. Janette Shofner, a very close friend, began coordinating meals for us. Every Monday, Wednesday, and Friday we received excellent hot meals (usually chicken and ham – always good). But I remember on one occasion, the Baileys brought steaks. Wow! They were awesome.

The food rotation lasted five months; friends, neighbors, and families from church helped out. We're so very thankful for their kindness. A group of friends got together and paid for a maid for Cathy. Neighbors mowed our lawn, bagged our leaves, and watched over our children. Friends helped set up Casey's birthday party. People even offered to buy our Christmas presents for us. The support was incredible.

God knew our needs and supplied people to meet them even before we knew we had needs. Ours was truly a community at its finest. But our most treasured gifts were words such as these: "We haven't forgotten you and your family, and we pray for you daily." Without question, God was honoring their prayers.

As we began our new life, taking care of Morgan quickly became overwhelming. She still screamed constantly. All of her intense crying caused her to sweat profusely, and so her hair was always wet. Morgan's knees were now curled up to her chest, and her arms and hands were contorted. Her right arm was outstretched behind her body with her hand in a fist. Her left arm was curled up next to her chest, and her hand and fingers were tightly clenched. Our precious little Morgan would drool, and her head and neck were turned to the left all the time. We would often sit behind her and hold her arms and legs down so she could try to relax. But holding her that way was very difficult.

Morgan's feeding schedule went like this: At 8:00 a.m. she had breakfast, noon was time for lunch, and at 6:00 p.m. she had dinner. She got 6 ounces at each feeding. Between meals, Morgan had to have snacks: 10:00 a.m., 2:00 p.m., and 8:00 p.m. Each snack took 45 minutes to complete. In addition, we were giving her insulin shots three to four times a day, and she received several types of medications, all of which we crushed and then placed in her feeding tube. It seemed like the machine was running and feeding Morgan continuously.

Someone was always with Morgan, usually trying to read a book to her, but most of the time just holding her hand and telling her we were there. We knew Morgan was in that tortured little body, and we just wanted her to know that we were there for her. My mom, Betty, was particularly good at talking to Morgan in a calm, soothing voice and telling her stories. Story after story and song after song, they would spend hours together. I know it was very hard for her to do, but what a nice break it was for us. Sometimes she would even take the night shift to give us a few moments alone together. She was a Godsend.

Bath time was quite the ordeal. It was as if we were bathing a 50-pound infant. Even as we gave Morgan her baths, she would scream at the top of her lungs and continue to sweat. Because of her constant sweating, keeping Morgan clean was an endless battle. At night, to put Morgan to sleep we tried several medications, but the only one that worked was chlorohydrate (the same medicine used to put a surgery patient to sleep). The dosage we gave her should have put Morgan to sleep all night, but it lasted only an hour and a half. I split the total amount available for the night into four equal doses, giving us six hours of sleep, starting at 8:00 p.m.

After Morgan would fall asleep, I'd work for the next 45 minutes straightening out her body and opening her hands. I had to do this very slowly so I wouldn't injure her muscles and tendons; if I straightened them too fast, they'd tear. Before long, Morgan would wake and start yelling again, and I'd give her more chlorohydrate. I'd then try to fall asleep around 11:00 p.m. to get some sleep before our next time for more medicine. At 4:00 a.m., my mother-in-law or mother would take over. This would give us a couple more hours of sleep.

Cathy and I would awake at 6:00, hoping that Morgan would not be screaming that day. But as we turned down a sound maker that Cathy had purchased to help us sleep, we could hear her screaming. Our hearts would sink, and we would both look at each other and say, "I don't want to do this another day." But we did, day after day; it never changed. Morgan didn't change.

On the Tuesday after bringing Morgan home, we started our first day of therapy. Somehow, we had to get all the kids ready for school and myself ready for work, get Morgan bathed and fed, and give her insulin shots and medications. We soon developed a pretty good system. Around 8:30 in the morning, Janette Shofner would pick up Kendall and Luke and take them to preschool. Casey would ride to school with a friend down the street. I would carry Morgan to Cathy's car and then follow her as we drove approximately 20 minutes to Children's Corner. When we arrived, I'd carry Morgan into rehab. She was curled up in a ball, so I'd put one hand under her shoulders and another under her behind. Throughout all this, Morgan would be screaming and yelling. I'd put her into her assigned bed, give Morgan and Cathy kisses, and then leave for work. Cathy was so brave. She stayed all day with Morgan helping the nurses and therapist.

Those days my work day was ending about 3:00 p.m. As often as I could, I'd try to leave early to help bring Morgan home from therapy. Before I'd leave the office, though, I'd get a call from Cathy with my daily Morgan update. As soon as my cell phone would ring and Cathy's caller ID appeared, I'd begin praying that Morgan had stopped screaming. But when I picked up the receiver, I knew that was not the case. As Cathy told me about their day, all I could hear was Morgan screaming in the background. It was unbearable.

By now we were desperate. The doctors suggested that we needed to eliminate any outside stimulation from Morgan: no noise, light, or touching as she lay in her bed at home. We placed heavy towels and curtains over the windows to make the room dark. We then had the other children be as quiet as possible. We even ate in an upstairs den instead of in the kitchen, which was next to Morgan's room. But nothing worked. Morgan just kept screaming and crying.

After a couple weeks of this, the doctors, therapists, and nurses offered little hope Morgan would get much better. The only hope given was that Morgan might be able to look at a board with pictures and communicate with her eyes. We would then be able to tell what she needed (drink, food, bathroom, etc.).

One night at about this time, I reached bottom, my lowest point. I sat outside on our front steps in the cold rain and just cried and screamed all by myself. I was angry and upset. I simply couldn't take it any more. I cried out to God to please help us. "Where are you?" I asked. "Why us? Please, Lord, lift this burden; it's too much."

I'm not proud of what I'm about to write, but I want to speak the truth about my heart. I truly had reached the lowest point when I began dreaming (day-dreaming as well as dreams at night) of how to die with Morgan. "She's in such agony, God; she can't live like this." I dreamed of drowning. I'd imagine putting Morgan in the front seat of my Camry, and together we'd drive down Pellissippi Parkway (a four-lane interstate). I could see us crossing over the Tennessee River, driving off the road, down the bank, and into the river. As the car submerged and the water rose, I'd imagine holding Morgan's hand as she screamed. As we drowned I'd still be holding her hand. Then as I took my last breath, I'd beg and ask God for forgiveness. Then it would be over.

Before Morgan's illness struck, I had never considered killing myself – much less Morgan. I'll never know for sure, but looking back at those moments, it certainly now seems that I may have been capable of it. In those awful days and moments of near despair, I did think about Cathy and the other kids, but my pain was so intense that they were almost an afterthought. It was all about me and Morgan and getting rid of the pain.

I felt this way for about a week. But God began to calm my emotions. He started putting men in my life that I could cry and talk with. This made a huge difference. People I worked with would come into my office and just cry with me. They began to take some of my pain from me. I later found that other men and women – some of whom I knew, others I didn't – were interceding in prayer on our behalf.

One night in mid-December Morgan became very sick. After we had fed her, she vomited. Then her breathing became labored, growing slower and slower, and she started gasping for air. We rushed her to Children's Hospital where they took x-rays to see if Morgan had aspirated. We sat in a small room waiting for the doctors to review the x-ray, and Morgan lay curled up in a ball, barely breathing. Cathy and I looked at each other from across the bed. "Cathy," I said, hesitantly. "Maybe it would be best for Morgan to die." No shock. No protest. Cathy just nodded yes, and we started crying and holding Morgan's hand and giving her kisses.

After about 15 minutes, the doctors returned and told us her lungs looked good. Within moments, Morgan began breathing normally. We were thankful that she was alive but so unsure of what tomorrow would bring. What we didn't know was that God's healing was right around the corner.

Many things happened over the next few weeks. People were constantly asking Cathy and me about our marriage. "Are you two okay? How's your marriage?" We were doing fine. We both tried to remain focused on God. Cathy was steady as a rock, but

I was on the wildest, most dangerous roller coaster ever built. My emotions would soar and then bottom out in the same afternoon. Despite all of the trials, the emotional highs and (mostly) lows, our marriage remained strong and soon grew even stronger. We were doing this together, with God as our focus. We knew God would not forsake us.

Now here's something I learned through all of this. Many times, in tragedies such as this, men "bug out" and leave their family. Before Morgan's illness, I couldn't understand how a man could do this. I've come to believe that in many cases he deeply loves his children and his wife, but the excruciating agony of the situation overwhelms him. He has to do something! He has two choices: Get free of the pain by escaping into the world of sin, drugs, alcohol, and/or sex; or go to the Lord on his knees and cry out for help and mercy. Even though I had thoughts of dying with Morgan, I never even considered running away from my responsibilities to my family by abandoning Cathy and the kids.

Cathy and I started reading a book called *Jesus Set Me Free*, by Delores Winder. It's a book about a woman who was miraculously healed by the Lord. Delores tells how the Lord completely changed her life. She describes how she began a relationship with the Holy Spirit and found out about His healing power. The book gave us hope, and our hearts began to change.

It was now mid-December and Morgan was still unresponsive. I asked the elders of our church to come to our house and to lay hands on Morgan and anoint her with oil (as described in James, Chapter 5). When they arrived, I was outside in a blue foldout chair on a beautiful day holding Morgan in my lap. There were about eight elders and they formed a circle around us. As they anointed Morgan with oil and prayed, Morgan just cried and screamed. As they left, I could see the pain in their faces. They were crying.

A couple days later, I received a call from a US LEC (the company I work for) sales rep in Chattanooga. Hunter was a brother in Christ, and he began to tell me about a man named Terrance Rose who, through the Holy Spirit, had the gift of healing. In just a couple days he was coming to Madisonville, Tennessee, to speak before a small congregation. Hunter had told him about Morgan, and he wanted to meet and pray with her. I quickly agreed. This seemed so crazy and contrary to most of the things I had learned in church. Yes, in the Bible it says to do these things, but this truly seemed off the "How to be a Christian" chart. A couple of other employees who are brothers in Christ decided to go as well, and on a Tuesday night we traveled one hour to Madisonville. I couldn't help but think this was like the story in the bible of the man whose friends carried him on his mat to see Jesus. When they arrived, they had to go onto the roof and dig a hole in it before they could lower their buddy to Jesus. Because of his faith and the faith of his friends, Jesus healed him that day, and I was faithfully praying that Morgan could be healed as well.

Terrance prayed for Morgan and then preached in the next room; he prayed over her again, and then he would preach. He must have done this five or six times. Finally, he told the congregation to get on their knees and pray for Morgan. You see, from the sanctuary you could hear Morgan screaming. In fact, we moved her two rooms away from the sanctuary, but you could still hear Morgan screaming through two doors and two sets of walls. We left the gathering that night seeing no apparent change in Morgan. I had imagined that she would walk out that night. But that was not to be. Still, I never felt this was a waste of time; something seemed to have changed.

Casey, my oldest daughter, by now had placed drawings all over my car, drawings of teddy bears with tears, with the following words: "PLEASE PRAY FOR MORGAN MOELLER, A VERY SICK LITTLE GIRL." I had one on each back seat window and one on the back window. One day as I drove to Chattanooga for work, I stopped at Krystal. As I pulled into the drive-through, the cashier saw the window signs and asked who Morgan was. I told her she was my daughter. As she handed me my order, she said, "I'll be praying for Morgan." Another time, while in Chattanooga after a meeting, I returned to my car. Someone had stuck to it a yellow sticky note that read, "I'm praying for Morgan." Those pictures meant so much to me. Thank you, Casey.

It was now getting close to Christmas, and Morgan was showing little or no change. Cathy decided to call a high school friend of hers who was a doctor. She asked him to check on other children who had suffered diabetic ketoacidosis (DKA) with cerebral edema. He agreed to call some experts and neurosurgeons in the Southeast. Late one night a couple days later, Paul called back when Cathy was asleep – his words dropped me to my knees. He told me there were very few cases of those who had survived and the best that the specialist he had talked to had seen was a young boy who could pull himself with the help of a walker. Most did not recover.

It seemed that when I was certain I could sink no lower, I did.

chapter seven

GOD'S MIRACLE ARRIVES:
GOD *and the* GOLDFISH

It was now a week before Christmas, and with Morgan's physical condition unchanged and the constant screaming, I was not looking forward to the holidays. Yet, Cathy and I were determined to make it the best we could for the other children, even though we knew it was not going to be a very happy Christmas.

By now we had found a place for Morgan that seemed to let her relax a little: on either Cathy or Grandma's lap. This was very difficult for both of them since Morgan weighed about 50 pounds. Before long their legs and back would ache and fall asleep. But Morgan seemed happier with them holding her, so they ignored the pain. Often, Morgan would fall asleep on Grandma's lap, so we had her take the afternoon shift. Sometimes, during Morgan's afternoon nap, she would relax and go the bathroom, and since the diapers didn't fit well, Grandma's lap would end up soaked. Grandma would just sit there with a smile on her face and say, "Oh well." We'd all laugh but Grandma wouldn't move a muscle so she wouldn't wake Morgan.

On Thursday, December 21, I happened to be home early from work. We were sitting on the couch talking and watching TV. Kendall and Luke were acting silly and playing in the den in front of Morgan. And then it happened: Morgan smiled! You could hardly see it, but it happened. Everyone started jumping up and down and praising Morgan. It was one of the greatest moments of my life. My daughter did something, anything – she smiled. Equally important, she actually looked at us, not through us.

The day Morgan smiled at us for the first time. December 2001

The rest of the afternoon was filled with joy. Kendall and Luke and I continued to do silly things to make Morgan smile. We danced and sang, Luke did front rolls, and Kendall stuck out her tongue. We did anything and everything we could to get her to smile. I quickly called the rest of my family and updated the

Christmas Eve 2001

hot line that night with the wonderful news. I still remember my mother coming over to the house and Morgan smiling at her. Mom smiled back and, through tears, said to me: "This is the best Christmas present ever. I don't need anything else."

A couple days later we celebrated Christmas. Our tradition was to celebrate with my family on Christmas Eve and then with Cathy's family on Christmas Day. Christmas Eve was tougher than I had ever imagined. Cathy's mom took Morgan into her room (our dining room) and sat with her as we opened our gifts. But all we could hear was Morgan screaming in the other room. We tried to ignore it, but we couldn't.

We kind of faked our way through opening presents, pretending to be excited for the sake of Morgan's brother and sisters. I was so very, very sad that Morgan was not with us. After we finished opening presents, I went in to get Morgan and had her sit on my lap as we talked. She was still smiling just a little, but nothing else had changed.

Later that night, as my parents were leaving, my dad looked at me and said, "Mike, next year

Opening presents with Cathy's sister, Angela, while Morgan screamed.

will be better. I promise." He gave me a big hug and put his arms around me. I hoped he was right and that things would get better.

During the week between Christmas and New Year's, we continued to do silly and crazy things to get Morgan to smile. It seemed to be working. Seeing her smile more often was a wonderful morale booster for us. Now she was clearly watching what we were doing, and her eyes followed us as we moved about the room. No longer was she just looking through or past us.

On the Thursday before New Year's Day, Morgan was in the den, and Cathy had gone into the kitchen for a minute, leaving Morgan propped up on the couch with some pillows. Luke, our youngest, now 2 years old, was eating cheese-flavored goldfish crackers. From the kitchen, and before she could stop him, Cathy saw Luke walk over to Morgan and put a goldfish cracker into her mouth. Cathy freaked out as she ran into the room. Morgan couldn't chew, but she *could* choke. Suddenly, Morgan started chewing on the cracker and swallowed. The celebration was on again at the Moellers.

Cathy called me at work and I headed home to see the surprise. When I arrived, Cathy put another cracker in Morgan's mouth, and she ate it. As we celebrated together, we started working with Morgan to see if she could do anything else. I asked her to stick out her tongue, and she did it. Another victory – two in one day.

Cathy then got a cup of Sprite and placed a straw in Morgan's mouth. She began sucking on it but had only enough strength to get the Sprite halfway up the straw. So, what do you do with a straw that's twice as long as it needs to be? You cut it in half. Cathy got a scissors and cut the straw in two. We watched and cheered for Morgan as the Sprite slowly made its way up the straw. Closer and closer until finally – success. Morgan had done it. She had sipped out of a straw. Halleluiah! Praise the Lord! Cathy started doing cheers for Morgan. I was jumping up and down, and the kids soon joined in. You'd have thought we'd won a million dollars.

After we calmed down, I asked Morgan if she could move her fingers or toes. I sat in front of Morgan and Cathy sat behind her to give her something to lean against. Morgan moved her right leg and put it against my chest. We all cheered her on. She did it a second time, but this time put just a little pressure against me. I pretended to fall backwards, and Morgan thought that was funny. She started smiling and even laughing a little. We played this game for another 15 or 20 minutes. What accomplishments! Morgan had chewed food, swallowed solids and liquids, and moved her leg – all in one day. The Lord had given me a huge slice of my daily bread. We praised God so much that day.

As we went through Friday and Saturday, Morgan continued to eat a little more each day. She was now eating the goldfish crackers, yogurt, and applesauce (every once in a while I'd sneak in a little chocolate treat). We were still feeding her Pediasure throughout all of this since she was really eating only a bite here and there.

On Sunday morning, we were getting ready to leave for church. Usually Cathy would stay home with Morgan, and the kids would go with me. They were loud and noisy – as usual – as I wrestled with them to get them dressed and ready to go. As we were about to leave, Cathy called to me to come into the bedroom for a minute. "Watch this!" she said. Cathy placed her index finger against Morgan's lips, and then I heard a very quiet "shhhhhhhh." Morgan had made her first controlled sound. Wow, what a present. I could have run to church that day.

At church I told everyone about Morgan's amazing progress. We rejoiced that day, as I told the story of how Morgan was now eating crackers and had said "shhhhhh." I could hardly wait to get home and hear it again.

What a surprise awaited us. Morgan had moved past "shhhhhh" and was now making letter sounds. She was struggling, but you could hear the letters as she forced her tongue to move and cooperate. By evening, Morgan was saying "Da-Da" and "Ma-Ma" again. Can you imagine how wonderful it was to hear my daughter say "Da-Da"? What a beautiful, beautiful sound.

The next day, New Year's Eve day, I was off from work. No holiday for Morgan, though; she had therapy. As I carried Morgan into the Center, Cathy called all the nurses over so they could hear Morgan's surprise. Ever so softly, Morgan said "shhhh" and then "Ma-Ma" and "Da-Da." Everyone cheered! Some of the nurses asked Morgan if she could say their name. She could, but very softly and in broken syllables. For example, Morgan would say "f-r-u-i-t." It was very soft but you could hear the sounds and make out the word. The nurses and therapist were totally amazed and overwhelmed.

As we continued through therapy, the speech therapist told us, "We'll get Morgan to speak louder; it's just that her diaphragm has atrophied." What?" I thought. "Morgan can scream your ear off; *volume* isn't the problem!" The therapist also told us "We'll be able to teach Morgan how to talk again in six to eight months." Cathy and I just looked at each other as if to say, "Yeah, right. Just wait to see what God is going to do." All the doctors, nurses, and therapists were wonderful. They had the best of intentions. In all their assessments and diagnoses, they were just trying to prepare us for the norm. But God had other plans that only He knew about and understood.

After returning home and eating dinner, we all sat in Morgan's room talking with her. By this time, Cathy's sister Angela and her fiancé Chris were at the house. The five of us (me, Cathy, Julia, Angela, and Chris) rejoiced at Morgan's smile and new sounds.

But more was to come. At around 6:00 p.m. things really started changing. Morgan began to speak a little bit louder, and her syllables ran together better. Over the next few hours, Morgan began saying full words and putting words together. We watched in amazement as God healed Morgan right before our eyes. We didn't dare leave the room to call anyone for fear we'd miss something. By 10:00 p.m. Morgan was speaking in full sentences. You'd have to be very quiet to hear her talk, but she was talking.

It was then that I heard the words I had dreamed of hearing for so many months: "Daddy, I love you." Oh man, I melted. I just sat there and cried with joy. We all cried as we were overcome with the magnitude of watching our daughter healed before our eyes. It didn't take 6 months for Morgan to start talking; it didn't even take 6 days; in less than 6 hours, God had Morgan talking and telling me she loved me. At that moment and through those words, God was telling me again that He loved me too.

You need to know that Morgan was still screaming and crying when she wasn't talking. That hadn't changed. But a lot of other things had. Because of all of Morgan's progress, later that night I decided to update the prayer hot line. I called to give everyone a New Year's surprise. The recorded voice mail went like this: "We have a big surprise for you tonight." I then put the phone up to Morgan's mouth and she said, "Go Vols." (The Tennessee Volunteers football team was playing in a bowl game the next day.) I then told everyone that the voice had been Morgan's, and I thanked them for their prayers.

As I went to sleep that night on the couch in Morgan's room, I dreamed of what the next day would bring. "If this healing continues, Morgan will be walking by Thursday." I went to sleep with more joy and thankfulness in my heart than I had had in years. All was well. We were praising the Lord and giving him all the Glory. I fell asleep saying, "Thank you, Jesus. Thank you, God. Thank you, Holy Spirit.

chapter
eight

THE BATTLE BEGINS:
MORGAN'S ANGELS
and the DEMONS

We woke up the next morning excited about what the day was going to bring. Based on the healing that had occurred the night before, who knew what was going to happen? "Morgan may be walking in the next few days," I thought optimistically.

Morgan was now speaking with us between her crying. It was wonderful talking to her, but she wasn't yet her old self. She was constantly praying and talking to God as though He were right next to her and was her best friend. When Morgan was talking, she was in constant prayer. "God, please heal me," she'd say. And in the next breath it would be "God, please let me die and go back above the clouds with you. Please take me to our special place." It wasn't as though she was saying this once or twice – it was a constant prayer and request to God. We were stunned and at a total loss for what to do, other than hold her hand. She would scream from the brain injury, and then she'd stop and say "Jesus, please let me die, but also take Mommy and Daddy and have your angels come take us above the clouds again."

Morgan's prayers lasted all day. This was proving to be one of my best days; I was overjoyed that Morgan was talking. On the other hand, this was one of Cathy's worst days. It was agonizing for her to hear Morgan repeatedly saying she wanted to die. Cathy was looking into her daughter's heart and seeing her pain and agony. Morgan was, for the first time, able to verbalize the agony she was going through, and it was almost more than her mother could bear.

I remember Cathy crying in the kitchen. As I gave her a hug, she said, "I give up. I can't do it anymore." This was the first time I had heard weakness in Cathy. She had been like Jesus' disciple, Peter; she was a rock. From the very beginning at the hospital when she had said, "We can do this; it could be worse," and throughout therapy when all seemed lost, Cathy was so strong. I could always look to her for encouragement since she was filled with joy and the faith that God was going to heal Morgan. But now the tide of grief and emotional pain had finally overwhelmed her. That she had lasted this long was a miracle in itself. Only by the power and comfort of God had she been sustained.

I, on the other hand, was looking at the physical side of Morgan. She was talking. Yay! Sure, the fact that Morgan wanted to die concerned me, but now she was talking. She was communicating with us!

Morgan continued to constantly pray, and we would hold her hand. As we watched and listened, I began to think about what was happening. "This is really odd," I thought. "Morgan hasn't once asked Cathy or me for help. Shouldn't an 8-year-old in such pain and agony ask her mom and dad to help?" But no. Morgan didn't ask us for help. Instead, she went in prayer straight to her Father in Heaven – her best friend. When Cathy and I could do nothing, He was right there listening to Morgan as His angels comforted her.

Then something truly astounding happened. Morgan started quoting aloud from the book of Revelation. I'm certain she knew little or nothing about this chapter of the Bible. Yet here she was, talking about how kings would bring their splendor into the new Heaven (Revelation 21:24). How did Morgan know this scripture? First she was praying to God, and now she was quoting scripture. This absolutely blew me away. But more was to come.

On New Year's night, around 9:00 or 10:00 o'clock, I was sitting on the floor in Morgan's makeshift bedroom with my head resting on the edge of her bed. Morgan was awake, and we were just looking at each other. It was a time that I had longed for. I was looking into my daughter's eyes and she saw me.

"Daddy, who's that behind you?" Morgan asked. Chills went through my body, and I got goose bumps all over. The wall was only a foot behind me, so I knew no one was there – at least no one I could see.

"Morgan, what do you see?" I asked carefully. She was looking right over my head as if seeing someone.

"Daddy, who's behind you?" she asked again.

"I don't know, Morgan. What's he look like?" I asked.

Morgan paused a little and then responded, "I can't really tell, Daddy." She was so calm; she just looked past me and wondered why I couldn't see what she was seeing.

"What's he wearing, Morgan?"

"I can't tell, Daddy."

"Morgan, do you think it's Jesus?" I didn't know what else to say. I was now feeling scared, a weird scared. I knew nothing was behind me, but I really didn't even want to turn around. Finally I did and saw . . . the wall.

Morgan thought for a couple seconds and then said, "Yea, I think so."

I was stunned. Neither of us spoke any further, and then Morgan stopped looking over my shoulder. "Is He still there?" I asked.

"No, He left," Morgan replied.

For another five or ten minutes we didn't move; we just looked at each other. I kept trying to understand or make sense of what had just happened, but nothing made sense. I then gave Morgan her medication and a kiss good night. Soon she faded off to sleep.

I went into the kitchen and told Cathy about what had just happened. Was Morgan dreaming? Had she been hallucinating? It was then we began to realize that something else was happening that we couldn't fully understand. While we had spent much of New Year's Eve praising the Lord and telling everyone how God was healing Morgan right before our eyes, she had been praying that God would let her die again and take her above the clouds. We were entering a new phase: not only were we fighting alongside Morgan in her physical battle, we were now fighting a spiritual battle for which we were not prepared.

The next day was very much like the day before. Morgan still prayed to God to heal her and take her away again above the clouds. She was still in a little ball with her arms all over the place and her hands closed in fists. Her knees were still up in her chest, and we had to hold her legs down so she wouldn't hit herself in the face with her knees. Morgan was still in pain and suffering, and she was still screaming all day long. Little had changed.

That night we had just finished giving Morgan a bath and were sitting on the floor of our master bath. Our backs were against the vanity drawers facing the Jacuzzi. As we sat there, we noticed that Morgan was staring over Cathy's shoulder at the left-hand corner of the ceiling. "Morgan, what are you looking at?" I asked.

"My angel."

"Where is he, Morgan? We can't see him."

"He's right over there Daddy." She was looking above the other sink in the bathroom.

Again, I had chills all over. This was really weird. You see, it's not like I don't believe in angels, but I figured they were off doing God's work helping *other* people. Now I realized they were here with *us* helping Morgan!

Wednesday morning we had an appointment with Dr. Zimmerman, another neurologist, to get a second opinion on the likely extent of Morgan's disability. We asked Jill Branson (one of Cathy's best friends and Scott's wife) to come and help us out. It was a cold day, so we had to hurry and get Morgan out of the car, into the wheelchair, and into the doctor's office. We arrived at the doctor's office with Morgan crying and screaming very loudly.

After only a few minutes, Morgan, Cathy, Jill, and I were led to a large consultation room. As we waited for Dr. Zimmerman to join us, Morgan began to look above a TV set against one of the walls and then started to talk to David, one of her angels. She asked God if he would "take me and Mommy and Daddy and Ms. Jill above the clouds back to Heaven." Jill was amazed. She knew it was happening, but now she was seeing it firsthand.

As Dr. Zimmerman entered the room, Morgan was still looking toward the wall and talking about David and her angels. Like the rest of us, Dr. Zimmerman looked over his shoulder to see who or what was behind him. He continued with his assessment, which turned out to be more positive than previously predicted. He told us that we would know in 6 to 12 months what Morgan would ultimately be like.

On Friday evening, a couple days later, we had just finished giving Morgan another bath. As we were drying her off and brushing her hair, she looked towards the shower and asked, "Daddy, who's that over there?" This time Morgan had a scared look in her eye. You could tell she was frightened.

"I don't know. What does he look like?" I replied.

Her description was totally unexpected. "He's black with red eyes."

Now *I* was scared. In fact, I was freaking out. Cathy and I just looked at each other. What should we do? This isn't stuff you learn about or talk about every day in church or Sunday school. We were clueless. We quickly got Morgan off the floor and left the room. As you can imagine, neither Cathy nor I slept very well. What had Morgan seen? What was going on? What should we do? Cathy and I asked lots of questions that night, and we prayed to God for protection and for wisdom.

On Saturday morning I decided we needed help. We didn't know what was happening with Morgan's angels and the demons. So I called our minister. "George, something weird is happening over here; I need you to come over and help us!" He then called our youth minister, Ron, and the chairman of the elders, Paul.

As soon as all three of them had arrived, I filled them in on what had happened New Year's night in Morgan's room, about her constant praying to God for healing and wanting to die, and about the past couple of nights with her angel and the demon she had seen. George asked Morgan questions.

After 15 minutes, we four men went into Morgan's bedroom while Cathy and Morgan stayed in the den. "Guys, what's going on here?" I asked. They each offered their thoughts. "Could Morgan be making this up?" "No way," I answered. "She's only praying to God. She hasn't asked Cathy or me for any help." Then Ron said something that made sense. "Mike, Satan's not happy with your family. You're all praising God and giving him the glory. You're under attack." Under attack? I didn't want to be under attack! I just wanted Morgan to get up and walk and get better.

While we were in the other room talking, Cathy was reading scriptures to Morgan. As Cathy read, suddenly Morgan began yelling. "Turn the Holy Book over. Turn the Holy Book over!" Cathy quickly closed the Bible and turned it over, but Morgan was still terrified. Then suddenly, she started screaming as if in horrible pain. Cathy yelled to me, "Mike, get in here!" I rushed into the den to find Morgan yelling and screaming in terror as she looked towards the fireplace. Cathy was trying to calm her, but you could tell Morgan was frightened of something.

"Morgan, what's wrong. What do you see?" Cathy asked.

Then Morgan said, "Mommy, Satan is right over there."

At that moment we remembered scripture that says, "Resist the devil and he will flee from you." We told Morgan, "You tell

Satan to run in the name of Jesus." Morgan then spoke these words: "In the name of Jesus, run." Suddenly, a calmness and big smile came over her face.

"Morgan, did he run?" we asked. She nodded and said, "Yes." Like a limp rag, I sat down on the floor by Cathy. I didn't know what to say or what to do. But after a couple minutes, we started praising and thanking the Lord for this victory. We had just faced our first battle. What we didn't know was that it was just the first of many to come.

When Cathy and I had finished praying, I went back into the other room and told George, Ron, and Paul what had just happened. I really don't remember their reaction because my mind was racing. "Did that just happen?" I asked myself.

In the meantime, Cathy was telling Angela, her sister, all about Morgan's angels and demons. Angela then told Shane, one of her best friends, about it. Shane and her mother and father-in-law were in prayer for our family and told Angela what we needed to do. "You need to anoint your home. As you anoint your home with oil, pray in the name of Jesus that the Holy Spirit would come in and fill each room and that anything not from God would leave the home and be bound and cast out." Matthew 16:19 ". . . whatever you bind on earth will be bound in Heaven, and whatever you loose on earth will be loosed in Heaven." Obviously, as I said before, what was going on here was not your typical Sunday school lesson or minister's sermon. This was beyond anything I could have ever imagined. But it was real and happening to us. We were under attack!

I was ready to do anything to bring peace and security back into our home. At about 10 o'clock Friday night, Angela came to our house. Along with her she brought some oil from Israel that she had picked up on her mission trip to Russia.

"Are you ready to get started?" she asked.

"Yep, I guess so." I was nervous, anxious, confused, and excited all at the same time. I was also unsure of what was going to happen. But none of that mattered. I was ready to do anything to help protect my family. "What do I do?"

"Just put oil on the entryways, door and window frames, and closet frames. Ask the Holy Spirit to fill each space and room and say that if there is anything that is not from God (yes, that means you Satan and demons) that they are bound and cast out in the name of Jesus." So we got started. We went through each room of the house, starting upstairs. Everyone was asleep, including Cathy, as we went into each room placing oil on the door and window frames and speaking out loud for the Holy Spirit to fill each space.

Honestly, at first I felt like an idiot. Rather than speaking out loud, I was actually talking quietly to myself. But, as I got going and went to my second and third room, I felt the Holy Spirit's presence. Suddenly I was speaking with authority and power. I had no idea where it came from, but it felt so awesome to be putting a whooping on Satan and his demons. The battle had already been won by the blood of Jesus. I just needed to claim the victory and cast evil out of our house, making it a sanctuary.

By the time we were finishing up, I was really getting into it! I was speaking louder and louder with the authority given to me by Jesus. I was so pumped up that night that it took me quite a while to go to sleep. But when I finally did fall asleep, I slept like never before since I knew there was a hedge of protection around our house.

The next morning, Angela asked if it would be okay for Shane, her family, and some friends to come over to our house on Sunday after church. Cathy and I quickly said yes, since they were coming to pray for and with us. We never turned down anyone who was willing to pray for us.

When the doorbell rang on Sunday afternoon, we greeted Shane and her husband, her mom and dad, and a couple of friends. There was something about them that brought calmness, but also a sense of power. We all sat in the den as Morgan talked a little but mostly cried and screamed as always. We told them about the past two weeks and all of the things that had happened. They weren't surprised. Instead, they began asking questions that no one had asked before, as though they understood what was going on. While some of them asked questions, others were in prayer over Morgan. I felt a peace that I can't describe.

After a couple hours of praying and talking about what Morgan had seen, they asked me if *I* needed prayer. I at first responded that I was okay, but then acknowledged that I really could use their prayer. So they gathered around me, laid their hands on my head and shoulders, and began praying and speaking what was on my heart. It was as if they were reading my mind. Suddenly it felt like a ton of bricks was being taken off my shoulders. I was crying uncontrollably as they prayed for my strength, my heart, my family, my marriage, and faithfulness for Morgan. It was then for the first time that I heard someone pray to God in a "prayer language." It was so soft you could barely hear it. It was as if a warm blanket had been placed on me as they prayed.

Then they prayed over Cathy with the same power and authority. When they had finished praying for Cathy, we talked a little while longer, and they told us what they believed was happening. "You and your family are under attack by Satan and his army. You must fight back in the name and blood of Jesus because it's His blood that Satan hates. It was Jesus' blood that defeated Satan, and he cannot stand against it." Our visitors, just as in Ephesians 6, had handed me my armor and a sword to fight the battle "against the spiritual forces of evil" we were facing.

Over the next few weeks, Morgan began telling us about her angels and about going above the clouds (where she says she went when she was "dreaming" in her coma). She talked of going to the beach and to the playground with her angels. Morgan told us she had three angels: David, Jacob, and UM. She would often have conversations with them in the house, car, doctor's office – almost anywhere. It was like she was talking to herself, but you knew it was a two-way conversation!

Morgan then told us about a brilliant and beautiful light with hundreds and thousands of colors. She said it made her feel so good when she was in the light. She told us that when she was there God told her, "Morgan, you are going to be healed; just wait." What could I say to that? God had spoken directly to my daughter, and the promise had been made that she would be completely healed.

As she retold the story, we'd try to trick her to see if she was making it up. We would ask, "Morgan, what did His face look like?" (We know by scripture that no one has seen God's face.) Morgan would respond, "I couldn't see his face." Morgan also told us she could see angels and demons fighting all around her. She could see the angels with swords, but they were fighting only darkness. Cathy asked if the angels had wings. "No, Mother, not mine." She told us the angels were her age and that they were boys with black hair and blue eyes.

In mid January, we were putting Morgan to bed one night. Suddenly she got a frightened look on her face and said to Cathy, "Mommy, you have snake bites all over your arms." We tried to convince Morgan that Cathy had no snake bites. We even turned on the lights and showed Morgan Cathy's arms. Then she looked at me and said, "Daddy, there's a snake on your shoulder." I still get chills when I think about it. That night, Cathy and I anointed our house again. We continue to do this over and over again as we feel led by the Holy Spirit.

chapter nine

GOD *is at* WORK: MORGAN WALKS *to* PAPA

We were now into mid January and fighting on two fronts: physical and spiritual. Even though Morgan was speaking at this point, she continued to cry and scream from the brain injury. Her body was like a ball as her knees were curled up and touching her chest. We still had to hold up her head, her arms weren't working, and her hands were still clenched in fists. On the positive side, Morgan was gradually eating more and more each day, but it was a chore to get food down her – she'd spit out the food as we fed her. Along with the hour-long feedings, we supplemented her nutrition with Pediasure, and we continued to give her an endless supply of drugs.

The side-effects of Morgan's daily requirements were beginning to show on our family. We started wearing down. Morgan con-

Playing outside
in the snow
with our family.
We threw
snowballs at
Morgan to make
her laugh.

January 2002

tinued to cry, but at least she was talking to us. She was also still seeing angels, and we were on our knees in constant prayer. Hundreds, perhaps thousands, of people prayed for us and Morgan, and we were still receiving food every other day from

our friends, church members, and neighbors. Even with all of this help and prayers, it remained an hour by hour, day by day, struggle. Through it all, however, we were so thankful that we had at least a part of Morgan back.

I remember telling myself that if she would just stop screaming we could make it. Her screaming was taking a huge toll on me. Cathy and her mom, on the other hand, seemed to be unaffected by the

Early January 2002

screaming. Finally, around the third week of January, Morgan stopped screaming. Praise the Lord!

As the screaming eased, however, Morgan began to weep tears of sadness and pain as her body was hurting. It was about this time that Morgan quit eating and had to be placed 100 percent on Pediasure. This was a real downer for us. We had started to believe that soon we would be able to take out the feeding tube. Patience was not and is not one of my virtues.

Pajama Day at therapy
Mid January 2002

This reminds me of something I learned during Morgan's sickness. I refer to it as "The deal Satan wanted to make with me regarding Morgan." Usually a day or two after Morgan had made some progress, she would take a couple steps backwards – kind of like "two steps forward and one step back." It seemed that it always happened right after I left a praise message on the voice mail. When I noticed the apparent connection, I remember thinking, "Maybe if I would just stop praising the Lord outwardly, Morgan wouldn't take steps backwards." That thought, of course, was just a trick, a lie from the father of all lies.

A couple weeks later (early February), Morgan started eating again. This time she did so well that we hardly needed the feeding tube. We felt like we could see the day coming when the feeding tube could be removed.

It was about this time when Morgan was measured for her "permanent" wheelchair. As part of the deal, the patient gets his or her name embroidered on the front of it for free. The nurse helping us asked Cathy what color thread we'd like for Morgan's name. Without hesitating, Cathy replied: "No need to put Morgan's name on the wheelchair. When we give it away, that person won't want 'Morgan' on their wheelchair." The nurses thought Cathy was crazy, but they humored her and again asked her what color she wanted. Cathy didn't budge. Seeing she wasn't going to pick a color, they gave up and gave in to "this crazy lady's" request.

In early February, Morgan's physical condition very quickly deteriorated. As a result of the brain injury, she began to develop a serious condition called "dystonia," a condition that causes the body to move uncontrollably. Morgan's legs would go straight and then bend, sending her knees into her chest in rapid fire (like a piston in a car engine). The rest of her body would also jerk out of control. This had been happening for more than a month, but by this point it was getting much worse. Morgan's knees would hit her in the chest and mouth so hard she would bleed from her mouth, and her teeth had loosened from the jarring. We'd have to hold down her legs to keep her from knocking her teeth out altogether.

This battering was taking its toll on whomever was holding Morgan. Most of the time it was Cathy; both she and Morgan had bruises all over them. Morgan's legs were moving out of control now every 10 to 15 seconds, and the movement was constant. It was very, very intense.

Late one Friday afternoon at therapy, Cathy told the head therapist, "I don't care what you have to do. We can't do this anymore. She's bleeding and she's bruising both of us; she's hurting herself and me as well. We need to give her more drugs or something." The therapist then told Cathy, "We've been talking about this. There's a surgeon in Houston who can help." The plan was to travel to Houston where they would conduct brain surgery and clip ("short circuit") the areas in the brain that were causing the "misfiring." As you can imagine, this was not the answer we wanted to hear. That night Cathy and I talked about the surgery, but we agreed that this was not God's plan. We both felt strongly against the surgery.

That night we went to the Lord as we cried out again for his mercy on Morgan. "God, Morgan is in your hands. You're the only one who can help. There are no more drugs, therapies, nothing short of surgery – please help us." We prayed on our knees into the early morning. We cried, begged, and pleaded as we held each other.

That was on Friday night. By Saturday the dystonia was 50 percent better. By Sunday, she hit herself maybe only once or twice in the face with her knees. It was unbelievable. It was another miracle. Once again God had come to the rescue when all hope was lost. Thank you, Lord!

Because the dystonia was significantly less, Morgan was more relaxed. I remember watching her sitting on the couch with her legs stretched out (not in a ball). I would get so excited that her legs were almost straight. Once again, God had given me my daily bread to keep me going. It was just the little things that I held onto. They were little changes, but they were huge to me.

To help out with therapy, we would play games at home. Usually, after Morgan's bath we'd put her on our bed. Then we'd sit beside her watching how long she could hold her legs straight before they'd bend. I'd hold down her legs and get them straight, and then she'd relax. As soon as I knew she was relaxed, I'd let go of her legs and we'd start counting. At first Morgan would make it for only 4 or 5 seconds, but over time this went to 10 seconds. I still remember the night we jumped from 15 or 20 seconds to 50 seconds. Then one night as we were counting, I kissed Morgan on her neck to tickle her a little. She jerked her head around (this was the first time she moved her neck, as it always faced her left side). We all cheered. Over the next couple of days, Morgan regained movement in her neck, and I got to give her plenty of tickling kisses on her cheek and neck.

To keep things going and to get some sleep, Cathy and I would take shifts with Morgan. Since Cathy had Morgan most of the day, I'd try to let her sleep during the evening. Besides, I could sleep anywhere, and if I was awakened, I could fall back asleep before my head would hit the pillow.

Morgan had improved enough by this point that we were able to move her back to her old room. She was very happy to get out of the hospital bed in the dining room and go back upstairs. During the night, I'd sleep in Kendall's twin bed, which was parallel to Morgan's bed (Morgan and Kendall shared the same room). During the night, Morgan would awaken several times.

On this one Wednesday night in mid February, Morgan woke up around 2:30 a.m. moaning in pain. There wasn't much I could do since it wasn't yet time for more medicine. I'd help her out the best I could, but she looked so uncomfortable with her knees curled up next to her chest and her right arm still stuck behind her. Somehow this night was different. I lay looking across a 3-foot span at Morgan in bed all distorted and with tears of pain flowing down her cheeks. We talked a little, but I mainly cried with her. I started praying to the Lord on my knees. "Father, I know you've healed parts of Morgan. But tonight, I need to know you're still in control here. I need my daily bread again. Please, Father, show me you're still in control."

After praying for around 30 minutes, I went downstairs and got Morgan some Motrin. I lay back down in Kendall's bed and continued my prayer: "Just something, God, please." About 5 to 10 minutes later Morgan suddenly moved her right arm from behind her back to her side. It was the first time she had moved her arm since the onset of her sickness. I almost fell out of bed. "Morgan, you just moved your arm," I said to her. "Can you raise it up?" I asked. She raised it up and started squealing with excitement that she could move her arm. I quickly came over to her bed and, like most dads, asked her for a high five. She honored me with multiple high fives!

Morgan had a rag that we used for her drooling. I handed her the rag and she started to wave it around like a flag and whooping it up. It was awesome. I quickly went into our bedroom to wake Cathy. "Cathy, wake up! You have to see this!" As I brought Cathy into Morgan's room, she continued waving the rag like a flag and gave Cathy high fives. It appeared that her arm was completely healed, perfect, like it had been before.

Having been privileged to witness this powerful scene, I sat down on Kendall's bed and began to weep uncontrollably. I realized in that moment that the Creator and Lord of the Universe had heard and answered my prayer – *my* prayer." It shocked me. Not that God had answered a prayer, but that God had heard *my* plea, *my* cries for help, and had come to *my* rescue. I was alone with Morgan that night and was the only one who had prayed that prayer. This was the night that changed my life.

By the time I came downstairs the next morning, Cathy's mom was up helping out with Morgan. I told Morgan to "show Grandma how you can move your arm." Morgan didn't move her arm. "Morgan, what's wrong?" I asked. She told me she couldn't move her arm. I then asked her, "Do you remember last night, giving me high fives and waving your rag?" "No, Daddy, I don't remember," she replied. I was crushed. What had happened?

Guess what happened the next morning around 3:00 a.m. You guessed it: more high fives, Morgan waving the rag like a flag, and Morgan moving her right hand as though it were completely healed. The next morning it was time to show Grandma the miracle, but once again, Morgan couldn't move her arm and didn't remember being awake.

Soon after that I understood what was happening. God was teaching me patience. "Mike, you need to be patient. I'm still in control." I believe with all my heart that God answered my prayers and allowed me to see (not once but twice, kind of like Gideon and the fleece) just a peek at what He had planned for Morgan's future. "After that, Morgan didn't move her arm like she did that Wednesday and Thursday night in February 2002. But we knew that this was a preview of the healing to come.

The next Sunday, Shane, Chad, Glen, and Sybil and Gary (friends of Cathy's sister Angela) came over to our house again to pray. This time it was later in the evening, around 6 o'clock. They were so excited to see what the Lord had done with Morgan. As they prayed over her, they prayed that there would be "More Gain" for Morgan. It sounded kind of hokey, but in fact, it was powerful.

As we continued talking, someone brought up the notion of generational sin. What was this? I had heard of it but never really thought about it. What of anything in my family or Cathy's family needed to be broken? I had no idea what Cathy's or my great, great, great grandparents were into going back seven generations. Also, what about Luke, our adopted son? What about his past generations? In the end, it didn't matter. They

Being silly with
Cathy, Angela,
Casey and
Kendall.

January 2002

Dressing for
Valentine's day.
Cathy gave
Morgan curls.

February 2002

Morgan
performs a
front roll.

February 2002

Morgan performing
her pretend pairs ice skating
routine at therapy.

February 2002

93

Cathy and Morgan play dress-up at therapy.
February 2002

Morgan at therapy.
February 2002

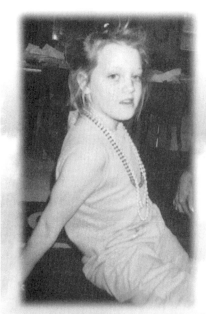

Morgan can finally sit up.
Late February 2002

Morgan in the "Stander" at therapy.
Late February 2002

laid hands on Cathy and me as we broke any ties to curses or evil from past generations. It was as if threads were being broken and a new legacy was being put into place. "As for me and my house, we will serve the Lord." Joshua 24:15.

Over the next few days, Morgan's physical condition improved greatly. In late February, on a Sunday night, Morgan asked if she could try to do a front roll. "A front roll? Morgan, you can't sit up yet," Cathy said. Undaunted, Morgan insisted that she be given the chance to try. So we placed Morgan in her ball on the floor. As she leaned forward, it happened. Morgan completed a forward roll

Morgan and special friends,
Anthony and Baby Charlie.
March 2002

and sat up at the end of it. We all jumped for joy. Morgan did front rolls again and again, each time getting better. One minute she couldn't sit up, the next minute she was doing front rolls and sitting up.

The next day was therapy. It was getting harder and harder to surprise the nurses because by now they had learned that Morgan would show up with something new and amazing she had learned the day before. She was making huge progress, especially on weekends and on Sunday night. So, when we went to therapy on Monday morning, it was show-off time. This day was no exception. The nurses and therapists cheered as

*Morgan and her
best friend, McKenzie.*

Morgan performed her front roll. It's the cheers and love consistently shown by these dedicated people that have made such a difference for Morgan and our family. We're so grateful for the continued dedication and love Children's Rehab Center has shown our family. Thank you!

Morgan's physical recovery accelerated. In early March, she wanted to try to walk across the room, so Cathy

supported her from behind with her arms around Morgan's chest. She supported all of Morgan's weight and let her barely lift her legs up and down to simulate walking. Morgan was very proud of herself. The rest of Morgan's body was starting to get better as well.

One day, while I was meeting with customers in Chattanooga, Cathy called my cell phone. I answered just to make sure nothing was wrong. "Mike, guess what. Morgan walked today in a special walker." I started crying as Cathy gave me the details. When I got

*Casey holding up Morgan
for their Easter Sunday picture.
March 31, 2002*

off the phone, I told the customer Morgan's story, and we all sat there together – me, my co-worker, and my customers – crying tears of joy. It was a very, very good day.

So, we watched in amazement as each day Morgan got better. Her arms and legs got stronger. We went to McDonald's one day, and I cried as I watched Morgan eat french fries and chicken nuggets by herself.

Each day, Morgan began putting more and more weight on her legs, but she still couldn't stand by herself. Morgan was making such rapid progress that the therapists soon gave up trying to figure out what was happening. They'd evaluate Morgan on Monday and come up with a plan for the next several weeks. By the end of the week she was past their goal. Eventually, they came to realize that they were watching a miracle before their eyes. Not surprisingly, they started calling her "Miracle Morgan."

On March 11th Morgan's feeding tube was removed for good. Yay! She continued to progress at an incredible pace. We couldn't wait to wake up in the morning just to see what God was going to do that day. Prior to the point where Morgan was ready to stand on her own, she and I made a bet. Here's how it came about. Cathy was painting the girls' toenails, and Morgan asked Cathy to paint mine. For fun I agreed. We all laughed, but I must admit, it wasn't a pretty sight: pink on one foot and purple on the other. It was

Morgan stands and rides her bike before walking.

April 2002

funny and Morgan laughed. "Tell you what," I said to Morgan. "I'll make you a deal. I'm not going to remove the polish until you walk." She agreed to take on the challenge. With spring and summer quickly approaching, however, Morgan needed to walk soon or I couldn't go barefoot or wear sandals anywhere!

Morgan struggles to take her first steps.

April 2002

By the end of March, Morgan stood by herself for the first time. We were outside in the driveway a couple days later when Morgan declared: "Mom, I want to ride my bike." Cathy smiled and said, "Morgan, you can't ride your bike; you can't even walk yet!" Morgan insisted, and so, based on what we had learned on other occasions about Morgan's strong will and God's wonderful grace, we decided to let her try. Once again, Morgan and the Lord proved us wrong. Off she went riding her bike 10 or 15 yards until she fell down in the grass. Once again Morgan proved us wrong – this time by riding her bike before she could walk.

Over the next few weeks Morgan got stronger and stronger. One day, after we took her to her first diabetes clinic, we headed for the parking lot of Children's Hospital. As we stood there beside our car, I asked Morgan, "Can you take a step toward me?" She slowly moved her right leg and took one small step before collapsing in my arms. Once again, another celebration of joy and praise. How far we had come! We quickly made a visit to my father, who had been hospitalized a couple days earlier as the result of a blood clot. When we entered the room, he got excited. "Papa, Morgan has something to show you." She stood there and then took a little baby step. "Praise the Lord!" he yelled. Those words of praise and joy were from his heart. He was so happy and full of praise to the Lord for what He had done.

Even though, technically, Morgan had walked, I hadn't yet taken off the nail polish. I wanted her to take a good five or six steps before the "de-painting." Then on a Friday night before the University of Tennessee football team's Orange-and-White game, it happened. We were working with Morgan and she walked across the room for the first time. We cheered and yelled. That night the toenail polish I had loved to hate came off for good.

The next day we had to show my mother (Mimi) and my father (Papa). We met Mimi at the Faculty Club on campus. She was so excited to see Morgan walk. But Morgan wanted to show Papa what she could do, because my father's prayers were to just see Morgan walk again.

When we arrived at the Orange-and-White spring game, I looked for Dad but couldn't find him. As UT's Assistant Athletic Director, he spent much of his time in the press box, but he wasn't there. Finally, we spotted him on the sidelines. It took us about 15 minutes to get Morgan down to the field in her wheelchair, but we finally made it. "What are you doing here?" Dad asked when he spotted us.

Just then, the first half ended, so Dad opened the gate and let us come onto the field. Morgan told Papa, "Go stand over there." She motioned for him to stand five or six feet away. When he was where she wanted him, Morgan got up out of her wheelchair and walked over to her Papa. His tears were flowing like rivers. He was so happy. As we celebrated, others came over, and soon we were having our pictures taken – Mimi, Papa, Casey, Morgan, and me with the UT cheerleaders. I hadn't let Cathy dress the girls so, to my embarrassment, they had on green and blue outfits while everyone else in the stadium was in Tennessee orange and white.

The day Morgan walked to Papa. Papa died five days later.

April 2002

Photo by:
John G. Karnes

Sunday morning at church was even better than usual: Morgan walked down the aisle. Our congregation stood in applause, and I held Morgan after she walked to me. Everyone was crying. God, the Great Physician and Healer, had delivered my daughter from death and now she was walking. How can I thank God enough for his great mercy on my family and me? Thank you, Lord!

But sometimes joy can be followed by grief. On Thursday (four days later), after spending several days with his grandson Brook at Wesley Woods (a school camp), my dad (a.k.a. Papa, Father, and the Colonel) had a massive brain hemorrhage. We found him still breathing but unconscious on the bathroom floor. We rushed him to the hospital, but there was nothing that could be done. That night my father passed away, but not before God had answered his prayer: "I just want to see her walk again." God granted him his wish and then took him to Heaven where today I know, without a shadow of a doubt, he walks with Jesus.

chapter
ten

Our Journey Begins: Morgan's Recovery Continues *and our* Transformation

It was late April – only a couple weeks later – when Morgan graduated from Children's Corner. It was a big celebration. Morgan had on a cap and gown as she walked across the room to everyone's cheers. We had snacks, cakes, cookies, pies, you name it. Almost everyone from Therapy who had taken care of Morgan came. I was so proud of her that day. What a great day!

Morgan's improvement continued at a rapid pace. People who weren't with her all the time couldn't see the day-to-day improvements, but Cathy and I saw changes daily. One day she couldn't sit at the table and feed herself; the next day she could.

One day she couldn't cross her legs; the next day, whamo, they were crossed.

As June arrived, Angela's (Cathy's sister) wedding was quickly approaching. As you will recall, within the first 48 hours in ICU, we had agreed on a goal that Morgan would walk down the aisle at Angela's wedding (this is when we didn't even know if Morgan would live). Morgan was able to walk across the room by now, but that was about it. Would she be able to walk down the aisle? Angela's wedding was outside, so that meant it would be a very long distance for Morgan to walk.

June 15 was the big day. All three of my daughters were drop-dead gorgeous, and Cathy was stunning. As Morgan started her walk as a junior bridesmaid, I started crying. She was so beautiful; it felt like a dream. Only eight months earlier she was on a ventilator and in a coma. Now, only by the grace and healing power of Jesus, Morgan was walking down the aisle. Praise the Lord!

Morgan walked about 30 yards, turned to the left, and walked 5 more yards, then she circled around the back of the outside seating and began her walk down the aisle. I don't think there was a dry eye in the crowd. We were all so very, very happy and thankful. God's timing is always perfect. Yes, it was Angela's day, but for us it was also a day of rejoicing in the Lord for so many wonderful things.

Morgan's recovery continued through the summer. Cathy, along with the homebound teacher, worked with Morgan to help her catch up on her schoolwork. In general, she had not lost that much time, but her short-term memory was an issue. Morgan had no trouble remembering what she had learned in school before she got sick, but she did have trouble remembering what she was currently studying.

Graduation Day from therapy at Children's Corner.
April 2002

Morgan walks down the aisle
at Aunt Angela's wedding.
June 2002

JDRF Walk-a-Thon for Diabetes.
Janelle is riding on Morgan's lap
with Kendall, and Daddy.

May 2002

Morgan and her friend, Janelle at JDRF walk.
May 2002

At the end of the summer, we went to Gatlinburg – and Dollywood – for a little vacation. I had dreamed of riding the roller coaster there with Morgan one more time. On this day, yet another dream came true.

Morgan rock climbing at her 9th birthday party.
July 28, 2002

In the fall, Morgan entered 4th grade. We took her out of private school and placed her in public school where she would have access to a full-time nurse. It was difficult for everyone at school, but they were supportive. Cathy and I weren't worried. We didn't expect a lot. We were just happy that Morgan was alive. Every day when I would drop her off at school, Morgan would limp her way up the sidewalk. It was tough for her, but she was doing it. Then, as I made my way around the exit circle, I'd watch every step Morgan made and would cry and thank God once again. Even today I still cry as I watch her walk into school. When someone who was almost taken away from you is given back, every day is a good day.

In the spring of 2003, Morgan decided she wanted to try soccer again. She was running now, but she was very shaky. Her coach and teammates were supportive, and many of her old friends were on the team. They helped her every day at practice. It was great for Morgan to be back out there with her friends again. This time, however, she wasn't the best athlete – she was one of the worst. But we didn't care. She was there. It was a miracle. Everyone knew Morgan's story, and we all cried as she kicked the ball the first time in a game. Everyone cheered her on: "Go, Morgan, Go!" It was music to our ears.

About this same time (spring of 2003), Morgan's short-term memory started returning, and in spring of 2004 she finished 5th grade. She still had issues, but in general, she was doing well in school. As she had once excelled at soccer, she had once been one of the best students with straight A's. Well, straight A's are no longer the norm; instead it's B's and C's. She improves every week and month, and her teachers continue to be impressed at her constant progress.

Today Morgan is playing soccer again and doing well. She walks with only the slightest limp. You really have to watch her to notice. Her right arm causes her problems, so Morgan learned to write with her left hand (she was right-handed before the illness). She'd prefer to write with her right hand, but it just won't cooperate. It's been a slow process, but she uses a word processor, a scribe, or a good old mom to complete most of her assignments.

About six months ago, Morgan was placed on an insulin pump to help control her diabetes. This has been a huge blessing since Morgan has more control over her blood sugar and more freedom with her diet.

As I come to the conclusion of this book, and as I think back on all that's happened, the story almost seems unreal – and I lived it! Writing it has brought back so many memories (some good and some awful) and so many tears. I remember Morgan as she was before she got sick: young, healthy, straight A student, incredible athlete, peacemaker in our home. I also remember what it was like after she got sick. In the Intensive Care Unit my prayer was simply for Morgan to live. When it became clear that she would live, I prayed that we would have just a little bit of Morgan back. When we got "a little" back, I prayed for her to walk. Now she runs.

On Sunday, April 16, 2004, we attended a University of Tennessee Athletic Department function on the football field at Neyland Stadium. It had been two years since Morgan had taken her first steps and had walked on the field at the Orange-and-White game to her Papa. As we hung out on the field, already painted for the next day's Orange-and-White game, listening to a band play, Luke brought me a miniature plastic football to play with. Soon Cathy and the other girls made their way to join us at the center of the field. With the lights on, we soon chose teams (three on three). It was me, Morgan, and Luke against Cathy, Casey, and Kendall. Luke snapped me the ball, and I pitched it to Morgan. She caught the ball and took off in her dress and bare feet, running all the way to the end zone. As she ran 60 yards for the score I cheered. There she was running down the field for a score on the same field that exactly two years previous she could hardly walk onto.

Morgan's spirit, drive, and determination continue to propel her forward. She knows that God's promise is to completely heal her, and, as she says, "It may be today, tomorrow, or the day before I die, but I know God's going to heal me completely." We're just waiting (most days patiently) for God's final miracle – the healing of Morgan's arm and diabetes.

We continue to be amazed at how God is using this miraculous story for his glory. Cathy and I speak regularly to churches, small groups, and schools. We want people to know that God is still in control and in the "miracle business." We want people to know that He wants to be our Savior and that he wants to give us "life more abundantly." God has a plan for our lives. Our life is like a quilt that's being knitted together. From our perspective, the back of the quilt looks like knots and tangles, but when we see it from God's perspective, the quilt is a beautiful pattern and His glory is revealed.

As you come to the end of the book, I hope you can see how God has transformed me and my family. The transformation is far from complete; it's a journey that will take a lifetime. I'm thankful for the transformation He made in my life, and I look forward to the new life He has promised.

You may be asking "How do I find this life that you're talking about?" "How can I be transformed by Jesus?" You need to know that you are not reading this book by coincidence. It was in God's plan before time began for you to hear this story. Know that His plan is great for your life. He has chosen you and knows your heart. He is calling you. "I stand at the door and knock; whoever receives me and opens the door, I will enter." Revelation 3:20. Jesus stands and knocks; you need only to open the door to your heart and invite Him in. The Gospel of Jesus is really simple: Jesus was a man, the only Son of God. He came as man and God, He died on the cross for our sins, and three days later He conquered Satan and death and rose again. And because he lives, we have an "Endless Hope" rather than a "Hopeless End."

If you want an "Endless Hope," just ask Jesus into your heart right now and pray something like this: "Father and Jesus in Heaven, I want to have Endless Hope. I want you to come into my heart and transform me forever. I am sorry for how I have sinned against you, and I repent of my sins and ask for your forgiveness. Jesus, I know you died on the cross for me, and I now ask you to live within me and change me forever. Amen."

Your destiny has just been changed, and now the transformation will begin.

So, now you – like the Moellers – are on a journey that will have good times and tough times. But the destination will be worth the ups and downs. I can't wait to go above the clouds and walk with Jesus. I want to say to the Father, "Show me, Father. Show me how you were glorified through Morgan's illness." And I know that when my dad (Papa) walks up to me and gives me a big hug, and when the many others whose lives were changed by Morgan's illness greet me, it will all be revealed, and I will see the beauty of the quilt that He was knitting all along.

APPENDIX

MORGAN'S DREAM COMES TRUE: SHE "HANGS OUT" *with the* PRESIDENT

I n January of 2003, Mike Bailey, the father of one of Morgan's best friends, asked me if a group called the "Dream Connection" could give Morgan a dream come true. The Dream Connection is a non-profit organization that makes dreams come true for children who have been through a difficult time or illness.

Mike, who knew Morgan's story and is a member of the Board, recommended that the organization make her dream come true. Mike and I had discussed this a couple times, but neither Cathy nor I felt right taking money from this great organization when we have been blessed financially. Mike quickly pointed out to us that "It's not about you; it's about Morgan." What we didn't know at the time was that it wasn't about money either; it was simply more of God's plan to continue to use our family for His glory.

Cathy and I finally told Mike that we would agree to allow the Dream Connection to grant Morgan her dream wish. Mike then told us he would like to come over to the house soon and ask Morgan what she wanted. Cathy and I thought it would be a good idea to first ask Morgan what her wish would be so she could think about it and be prepared to give Mike an answer. So, one night when Cathy was putting Morgan to bed, she told Morgan about the Dream Connection and that she should be thinking about what she would like to have for her "dream." She calmly sat there and thought for a minute.

"Mom, I know what I want," Morgan said.

"What do you want, Morgan?" Cathy asked.

"I want to go back above the clouds and be with God again." Wow! How do you respond to that? It had been more than a year since we had talked to Morgan about her experience of looking into Heaven and God speaking to her. And now, suddenly, Morgan teaches us what's important. "I want to be with God." Morgan knows and has seen the beauty and peace of Heaven and the incredible feelings of being with God. She wanted more than anything to return to God's presence.

Hardly able to answer, Cathy told Morgan that we did not want her to go back to Heaven just yet and to think about what she would like second best. Morgan quickly answered. "I know what I want." Cathy, amazed at the quick answer, asked what her second dream would be. "I want to meet George, George Washington."

"George Washington is dead, Morgan," Cathy replied.

"No, not George Washington," she said. "I want to meet George Bush, the President."

This seemed very odd. Morgan doesn't follow politics, but for some reason – God's reason – she wanted to meet the President. A couple days later I asked Morgan, "Why do you want to meet with the President." Her answer was simple, sweet, and innocent. "I just want to hang out with him." We all started imagining a night with the President. Morgan would be sitting on his lap just hanging out, and the rest of our kids would be putting on a play or doing a fashion show for the President and Mrs. Bush. The Bushes would be in for the treat of a lifetime!

The next day we told the other kids in the van about Dream Connection and that Morgan could have anything she wanted. Casey, Kendall, and Luke quickly started giving Morgan ideas. Suggestions ranged from a trip to Atlantis in the Bahamas, to Disney World, to Hawaii, to a pony. Morgan just smiled and stayed focused. She wanted to meet with the President.

On Thursday, a few days later, Mike Bailey came over to our house to talk with Morgan. When Mike asked Morgan what she wanted, she told him, "To go above the clouds and be with God again." Mike gave her a great answer. "We don't want you to go just yet, and God will take you there someday again." Morgan then told him her second wish: to meet the President. Mike was surprised at the request but answered as positively as he could. "That sounds pretty cool, Morgan. We'll see what we can do." I think Mike left touched in a very special way that night, having offered a 9-year-old child anything she wanted and getting an unselfish response.

Mike and the Dream Connection started working on Morgan's request. This was a unique one that would take time and connections. Over the course of the next year, many people were involved with letter writing, phone calls, and meetings to make Morgan's dream come true. A couple months after Morgan's meeting with Mike, we received a letter from the White House telling us that the President would try to find time to help. Then silence for many months. We figured it had just died there.

But God was putting the final touches on the plan.

Suddenly, the week after Christmas 2003, Mike Bailey called me with some news. He asked me, "What are you all doing on Thursday and Friday of next week (January 9 and 10)?" I said I'd be out of town on business. Mike told me that the President was coming to Knoxville then and that there was an outside chance Morgan might be able to meet him. Mike had me tell Cathy but not Morgan so she wouldn't be disappointed if it didn't work out.

Cathy and I then kind of put it in the back of our minds until we got Mike's next call (Monday). "This is coming together, Mike, and it may happen. It looks like Morgan will get to meet the President on Air Force One just before he takes off on his way out of town. It'll be just Morgan, though." To be honest, Cathy and I were a little bummed. Our ideas of hanging out with the President had turned into a short hello on Air Force One for Morgan! We stayed positive, but we weren't as excited as we were before.

On Wednesday things really started heating up. Mike was calling often providing updates. Now things had changed, and she was going to meet the President at the Knoxville Convention Center after his speech. It was really going to happen! The Wednesday before the President was in town, Jack Bailey did the run-through for our family to simulate the next day. It was pretty much set. We were on the President's schedule, and we were now going to have a couple minutes with President Bush.

As Cathy and I talked about the new plans, I told her she ought to go to Morgan's school and tell her the great news. Cathy agreed and took Morgan out of class to tell her what was planned. Morgan was ecstatic. She was so excited she started to cry, then she yelled with excitement, and then she went back into her class to spread the news. I know it was one of Morgan's best days, but the real best day was yet to come.

As our friends started finding out that Morgan was going to meet the President, we began getting requests for his signature on ornaments, books, or just a piece of paper.

Cathy and I started asking Morgan what she was going to say to and ask the President. Morgan thought for a little bit and said, "I don't know." But the more Morgan thought about it, the more she wanted to talk to him about God, Jesus, and her diabetes. This was really cool coming from our daughter. Here is my 10-year-old daughter who just wants to tell the President of the United States about God. Well, Morgan would get her chance the next day – Thursday, January 9.

That night there was calmness in our house – a peace that I'm unable to describe. Yes, we were excited, but the kids went right to sleep, and Cathy and I were not anxious or nervous about the next day. I thank God for the calmness and peace in our home that night.

The next morning we all slept in a little since we didn't have to be at the Convention Center until 11:00 a.m. The house was filled with excitement as the girls struggled to find the perfect outfits, hairdos, and nail color. Luke wasn't at the house, since we had decided we wouldn't take him. He was, after all, a 4-year-old little boy. Need I say more? Later, we found out this was a wise decision since we had to wait several hours until the President's speech was finished before meeting with him.

I talked to Mike again at 9:00 and we were all set to meet him at his office at 10:00. Mike then chauffeured us to the Convention Center is his wife's Suburban. On the way, we picked up Jack Bailey, who had represented our family the day before on the dry run. We were running a little late, but we were still okay. Security at the Convention Center was tight, and there was a buzz everywhere. Mike dropped us off and wished us good luck.

Jack took us inside, where we were soon stopped because we didn't have name tags. (The event was a fund-raiser and con-tributors paid $1000 a plate lunch to attend). Jack got on the phone right away to his White House staff contact, Davis White, who promptly showed up to help us out. Davis was only 26, very nice, cordial, and good-looking (according to Cathy). He led us upstairs where paying guests were waiting in line to pass through metal detectors at the security point. Davis took us to the front of the line and kindly told those in line that he needed to get us in quickly: "They're dignitaries here to meet with the President." After that introduction (and a thorough search), we passed right through.

Davis escorted us to our table, right up front. Facing the stage, we were on the left side next to the curtain and Secret Service. We had some of the best seats in the house. Next, he gave us some of the details of the plan. After the President finished his speech, Davis would quickly take us behind the curtains to a room backstage where we would wait for the President.

We took our seats and got comfortable at the table for a long wait. It was only 10:45 and the President was not scheduled to speak until around 1:00 p.m. So, for the next couple hours we just hung out and tried to look important like everyone else.

We could see that Morgan was starting to get a little nervous about meeting the President. Cathy tried to reassure her by telling her that the President is just another daddy and that he has two daughters. She encouraged Morgan to think of him that way.

To pass the time the kids started saying that they were going to call the President "George" or "GW." Cathy was mortified and told them the only way they would be responding to the most powerful man in the world was "Mr. President."

The President started his speech around 1:00, and it lasted 15 to 20 minutes. He really did a great job. I have Morgan on video right before the President's speech. She and Jack Bailey had put together an American flag made with little stars that had been part of the table decorations. In truth, Morgan was bored and ready to meet the President.

As the speech appeared to be winding down, we saw Davis coming towards our table from the back of the room: it was show time! Suddenly I found myself nervous and my adrenaline running. We gathered our things and got ready to move, but the President talked for another 5 minutes before concluding. Then people began coming toward the front to shake the President's hand.

So that we wouldn't miss the President if he didn't shake hands long, Davis rushed to get us behind the curtain and to our own room quickly. (The room was just a small one in the Convention Center with a curtain and a table – nothing special.) We took off our coats, took a deep breath, and got settled in to wait for the President. Davis stood outside watching for him to come down the hall. I had my video camera ready, but much to my dismay, I had forgotten to charge the battery the night before. I was so concerned the battery would run out, I almost made myself sick worrying about it.

Soon Davis gave us the nod that the President was coming. As we moved away from the table to the center of the room, he walked around the corner with a big smile on his face. He didn't have a gang of Secret Service agents or his usual entourage with him. He had told his staff he wanted to be in the room alone with us. I thought that was pretty cool.

As he approached, he stuck out his hand and asked, "So, which of you is Morgan?" He shook her hand and then shook my hand as I introduced myself. I stepped back and got my video camera rolling. He chatted with Morgan for a little bit and then asked who else was with her. He shook Casey's hand and then Kendall's. Kendall was scared to death but very, very cute. He shook Cathy's hand and then said to Morgan, "Let's get some pictures." I handed my video camera to one of the photographers on his staff, and he continued shooting our meeting.

After another staff photographer took several still pictures, it was autograph time. The President pulled out a Sharpie and

autographed Casey's cast (she had broken her arm earlier in the week). We then asked him to auto- graph an ornament for Morgan's teacher, Mrs. Coleman. When he fin- ished the autograph he told Morgan, "I hope this gets you an A." After he finished signing some more autographs, we chat- ted for a few moments.

Morgan's dream comes true. She "hangs out" with the President.

January 2004

As our time was ending with the President, I asked him if he would do us a favor. Without hesitating, he said, "Sure." I then asked the President, the most powerful man in the world, if we could pray with him. I think he was a little surprised that we asked, but he quickly said, "Yes, let's do it."

Our family circled the President. I stood on his left side and Morgan held his right hand. I told the President that his broth- ers and sisters in Christ loved him and wanted him to know that he was doing a great job and that he should keep it up. He smiled and thanked me.

Then, with my right hand on his shoulder and my family circling the President, I prayed for God to bless him with the wisdom, knowledge, and peace that only God can bring. The prayer last around 45 seconds, but it was incredible. I really don't remember much of what I said, but I remember looking at him as we prayed. Here was the most powerful man in the world leading the most powerful nation bowing his head to our Lord Jesus Christ. Wow!

After the prayer, he smiled and kindly said goodbye. He walked out the door and waved as he left for the airport with his entourage following. We were the only ones left behind watching him leave. What a moment for all of us to remember.

Later, I thought about our time praying with the President. At that moment, I realized that the ground at the foot of the cross truly is level. It doesn't matter who we are or what we do, Jesus loves us, and we are all equal when it comes to God's grace.

We found our way back into the main area of the Convention Center where we met up with Jack and Joe Bailey. As I understand it, Joe was the guy who really made this happen. I can't thank him enough for what he did to help make Morgan's dream come true.

Many people ask, "What did the President say? What was he like? What did Morgan tell him?" The answer to the last question is really simple: "We just hung out with him." That was what Morgan wanted to do. But I believe God placed us there that day to pray with the President and to begin another part of our journey with God.

That afternoon, the radio, TV, and newspapers found out about Morgan's Dream meeting with the President. She was on the radio that night. The next day (Friday), a TV crew came to the house and interviewed Morgan. We were able once again to tell the story of Miracle Morgan and the faithfulness of God. The TV station aired the story later that night. To my amazement they didn't take God out of the story.

A newspaper reporter also interviewed Morgan on Friday. As the reporter left, I asked her when the article would run. "Tomorrow," she answered. Since she usually writes for the religious section, we figured the story would be buried inside the paper. To our surprise, however, Morgan was on the front page of the *Knoxville News Sentinel* on Saturday. There she was, my beautiful daughter smiling with a picture of her and the President. It was awesome! The article was incredible and perfect. God was exalted and glorified. *Sentinel* reporter Jeannine Hunter did a great job.

So Morgan's dream had come true. As Mike Bailey said, except for some gasoline and cell phone charges, it didn't cost the Dream Connection a dime. But the memories will last forever. I know God's hand put this together. It was too perfect for any human to pull off. I think God wanted our family to pray for the President, and that's why Morgan's dream was to meet him and "just hang out."